THE
MOUNTIES
MARCH WEST

The Epic Trek and Early Adventures
of the Mounted Police

TONY HOLLIHAN

FOLK
LORE
PUBLISHING

© 2004 by Folklore Publishing
First printed in 2004 10 9 8 7 6 5 4 3 2 1
Printed in Canada

The Publisher: Folklore Publishing
Website: www.folklorepublishing.com

National Library of Canada Cataloguing in Publication

Hollihan, K. Tony (Kelvin Tony), 1964–
     The Mounties march west : the epic trek & early adventures of the mounted police / Tony Hollihan.

(Legends series)
Includes bibliographical references.
ISBN 1-894864-04-2

     1. North West Mounted Police (Canada)—History. 2. Northwest, Canadian—History—1870–1905. I. Title. II. Series: Legends series (Edmonton, Alta.)

FC3216.2.H64 2004   971.2'02   C2004-901929-5

Cover Image: NWMP figure by Ewa Lament.

Photography credits: Every effort has been made to accurately credit the sources of photographs. Any errors or omissions should be directed to the publisher for changes in future editions. *Photographs courtesy of* Glenbow Archives, Calgary, Canada (p. 10 & p. 72, NA-47-1; p. 29, NA-1406-214; p. 40, NA-742-1; p. 50, NA-2730-1; p. 76, NA-47-3; p. 84, NA-3173-9; p. 86, NA-47-9; p. 96, NA-47-5; p. 112, NA-47-12; p. 141, NA-249-1; p.177, NA-2446-11; p.192, NA-3811-2b; p. 196 & p. 228; NA-40-1; p. 198, NA-302-1; p. 202, NA-343-1; p. 205, NA-659-22; p. 211, NA-1407-1; p. 221, NA-98-13; p. 223, NA-23-3; p. 225, NA-40-1); National Archives of Canada (p. 13, C-6513; p 19, C-2775; p. 54, PA-28146; p. 64, C-4953; p. 139, C-4164); National Library of Canada (Title page, C-62548; p. 45, C-17038; p. 81, C-62596; p. 94, C-3398; p. 121, C-62549; p. 127, C-62596; p. 132, C-62629; p. 157, C-62665; p. 169, C-62679; p. 225, C-66055).

We acknowledge the support of the Alberta Foundation for the Arts for our publishing program.

The Alberta Foundation for the Arts   **Alberta** COMMUNITY DEVELOPMENT

COMMITTED TO THE DEVELOPMENT OF CULTURE AND THE ARTS

PC: P5

TABLE OF CONTENTS

Dedication

FOR LAUREEN

Prologue

THE FALLING SUN WAS NEARING the flat prairie horizon on a late spring day in 1873 when Abe Farwell saw the yellowish cloud of dust blossoming to the southwest. He stood for a moment and dragged a ragged handkerchief across his sweaty brow. He could tell that whoever was kicking up the dirt was headed towards the Cypress Hills where Abe had a trading post known as Fort Farwell.

"Hey Alexis!" he called. "Get on out here."

Alexis Lebombard, Farwell's interpreter, was busy inside one of the fort's palisaded huts preparing bales of furs for transport to Fort Benton, Montana. Lebombard made his way over to Farwell.

"What do you make of that cloud?" Farwell asked, pointing to the southwest.

"Movin' pretty fast," Lebombard replied. "We'll soon know what they want. They's coming this way."

"Yeah." Farwell paused thoughtfully. "Those boys are in too much of a hurry to be traders," he finally said. "You go inside the post and get a rifle. Keep your eyes on 'em when they get here. Last thing we want is trouble."

Lebombard grunted, turned and headed back inside.

"I got a bad feeling 'bout this," Farwell muttered to himself and continued loading the furs onto his carts.

The trader's intuition was right. The men riding towards the Cypress Hills were an ornery collection of 13 wolfers out of Fort Benton, known as the Green River Renegades. The Renegades made their living by poisoning wolves, a profitable business because of cattle barons who, eager to get rid of the vicious predators, paid the renegades a bounty of $2.50 a hide. With so many wolves on the prairies a wolfer could pocket a few thousand dollars in a year.

Wolfing profits were also high because overhead was low. Buffalo meat and strychnine were the tools of a wolfer's trade. A wolfer would kill a buffalo and douse its carcass liberally with the poison. Then he only had to wait for the wolves to arrive and chow down. They always did. It was easy work and attracted the dregs of society—those who took pleasure at the sight of suffering. Wolfers were despised by just about everybody, but especially by the Natives, who often found their dogs poisoned. The dogs were important beasts of burden in any Native camp.

It didn't help that the Green River Renegades were mean characters even when they were in a good mood. And as they approached Fort Farwell their mood was anything but good. After a drunken spell in Fort Benton where they had enjoyed the returns of a long, cold winter hunting wolves, they discovered that 40 of their horses had been stolen. There was little more important than a horse on the plains, and in the minds of many westerners, a man could rightfully dole out just about any punishment to a horse thief. In the minds of the Renegades, only death was appropriate.

The Renegades quickly assembled a posse. With bloody revenge in mind, they tracked the thieves north to the Canadian border, where the trail went cold. They decided to head for the Cypress Hills, on the eastern fringe of Whoop-Up country, which was the booze peddler's paradise. About a dozen trading posts or "forts," including Abe Farwell's establishment, occupied the area. The term "fort" was a flattering description for the collection of rickety old buildings with palisades of sharpened logs. The forts dealt mostly in booze and rifles, and the Renegades rightly figured that if they couldn't find their horses, they could at least get drunk.

"Howdy, boys," called Farwell, as a pair of them rode up to his fort.

"Aft'noon," grunted John Evans, one of the Renegade leaders.

"Don't see no furs." Farwell scanned the men. "What brings you up this way in such a hurry?"

"Looking for some damned horse thieves," came the reply. Evans explained what had happened.

"Hear there's some Injuns up around these parts," said Thomas Hardwick, another of the leaders.

"Just some Assiniboine," said Farwell. "But they can't be the thieves you're after. They been here all winter. I'd wager they don't have four horses, let alone 40. They been begging on and off 'round here for months."

Evans and Hardwick spoke to each other and turned back to Farwell.

"Tom'll be spending the night here. I'll be back with the boys tomorrow. Make sure you got some kegs ready."

Evans rode back to his men, and together they headed to the other forts in search of better news.

Breakfast was barely finished the next morning when the Renegades returned. They gathered around the rough, whipsawed tables inside the post and advised Farwell to make sure they never saw the bottom of their cups. Other thirsty folk soon joined them.

"Name's Hammond," introduced one of the newcomers. "Hear you folks are from down Benton way."

"Yup. Looking for some horse thieves."

"You boys come to the right place then," Hammond replied. "This place's maggoty with 'em."

"What's that?" asked Evans, his interest suddenly peaked.

"The redskins around here are born horse thieves," he replied. "I just had to give one a couple o' gallons of whiskey and a plug of 'baccie to get my horse back. Claims he found it. Not bloody likely, I says. Now the horse's gone again. You can bet the Injun liked the deal so much, he came back for more."

"You don't say," said Evans.

Farwell, who overheard the conversation and feared its outcome, interrupted. "George, you danged well know there's no way of knowing who took your horse. The cursed beast spooks and flees liked a scared prairie dog."

"Everyone knows the redskins are born thieves," objected Hammond. "I know he took it, alright."

The Renegades nodded and muttered in agreement. It was all the confirmation the drunken men needed.

"Boys, I think we should take care of this problem in our own way," said Evans. As the men left, Farwell went ahead to the Assiniboine camp, hopeful he could head off any violence.

The Renegades crossed the narrow stream that would become known as Battle Creek after this day, and soon came upon the Natives' camp. Evans directed them to position themselves on a small coulee overlooking the scattered collection of tipis. Then he rode into the camp, somehow managing to stay in the saddle in his drunken state.

"Where's our horses?" he demanded.

"No horses," came the terse reply from an elderly Native.

Evans looked around. He couldn't see any horses. He could see Farwell and glowered at him. He turned and rode back to the coulee.

Farwell was trying to convince a small group of Natives of the seriousness of the situation, but they had also been drinking, and in that state, communication was difficult.

"You know me. I'm your friend," he said again. "These are bad men, wolfers from Montana. They think you have their horses. Now, I know you don't, but if we don't do something, there's gonna be bloodshed."

"What we do? We not have their horses."

"Have you got some you could give them? Anything?"

The Natives were silent.

"They've got rifles and lots of ammo," Farwell added.

"Don't like deal with wolfers," one of the braves finally replied. "Ask what they will take."

Farwell rode back to Evans.

"Evans, listen," he began. "You can see these Indians don't have your horses, but—"

Farwell fell silent when a shot rang out. He looked around, but couldn't tell who had fired it. No further discussion occurred as a hail of bullets rained down on the camp. The Assiniboine let loose a volley of arrows and the occasional ball from a muzzle-loading musket. The defense was ineffective against the Henry and Winchester repeaters of the Renegades. Farwell watched as the booze-fueled outlaws slaughtered nearly everyone.

With victory assured, the Renegades made their way into the camp. Women who failed to flee were captured and raped throughout the night. The few remaining braves who tried to defend them met with a quick end. With bloodlust riding high, the wolfers turned to bludgeoning their helpless victims. An old Native named Wankantu was among the last to die. After the wolfers had clubbed him to death with a hatchet, they decapitated him and impaled his head on a spike outside nearby Fort Solomon, a grisly reminder to all not to mess with wolfers. Back at Fort Farwell, they buried Ed Legrace, the only wolfer to die. The bodies of some 30 Assiniboine who were killed were left to rot in the heat of the day, easy and welcome meals for scavengers.

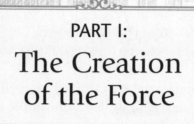

PART I:
The Creation of the Force

CHAPTER ONE

A Vision and a Need

ON A CLOUDLESS LATE NOVEMBER DAY in 1869, when the last leaves dappled the trees fiery orange and dark purple, Prime Minister John A. Macdonald stood in his parliamentary office before a map of British North America and smiled with satisfaction. The map identified the recently created Dominion of Canada. Granted, it was hardly an imposing sight: a modest strip of land that surrounded the St. Lawrence Valley, followed the St. Lawrence River south and branched tentatively west along the northern shores of the Great Lakes. But the creation of the Dominion had been an achievement some considered unlikely, and Macdonald could reflect with pride on his determination and political skill that brought together the four former British colonies in the years leading up to July 1867.

But as Macdonald's eyes wandered along the map to the territory west of the Dominion, he knew his work was incomplete. His grand vision for Canada saw the small country in the northeast of the continent stretching from sea to sea. The vision demanded a change of heart in the Pacific colony of British Columbia, which had rejected the terms of Confederation.

Macdonald realized that it would be difficult to entice British Columbia to enter Confederation as long as it remained isolated, thousands of miles distant from the Dominion, but he considered the problem surmountable.

The vast region that linked the westernmost province of Ontario to British Columbia was called Rupert's Land, and it had belonged to the Hudson's Bay Company (HBC), the great British fur-trading operation, since 1670 when Charles II granted the HBC exclusive trading rights in the territory. As ownership of Rupert's Land was necessary to ensure a transcontinental nation, Macdonald's Conservative government had opened negotiations with the governors of the HBC in 1868 for its purchase. In March 1869, they reached an agreement. The governors were tough bargainers, and the deal cost the Dominion £300,000, millions of acres of land and a guarantee that the HBC could continue to trade in the region. As per the 1868 Rupert's Land Act, the HBC surrendered Rupert's Land to the British Crown, which in turn would transfer it to Canada. To prepare for that transfer, the Dominion Parliament passed "An Act for the Temporary Government of Rupert's Land and the North-West Territory" in June 1869. Macdonald saw the territory as a Canadian colony under the direction of a lieutenant-governor and council appointed by the Dominion government, until a larger population justified self-rule and, eventually, provincial status.

While Rupert's Land provided the necessary link with British Columbia, it was valuable in its own right. For generations Britain's overseas colonies had exported natural resources and imported manufactured goods, thereby strengthening the British economy. Macdonald anticipated that Rupert's Land could serve a similar purpose for Canada. Settlers would till the soil to plant and sell crops and then use the profits to purchase goods. Sales would strengthen commerce in the provinces, where manufacturers and industries

John A. Macdonald (1815–91), the prime minister of Canada whose vision led to the creation of the NWMP

were located. And a burgeoning economy would please voters, ever a concern for Macdonald.

But other political considerations emphasized the need to fill the West with settlers. The United States had expressed an interest in Rupert's Land. In the late 1850s, Minnesota politicians and businessmen had advocated expansion into the northwest. Rumors suggested the construction of a transcontinental railroad near the United States' northern border, designed in part to siphon trade from Rupert's Land and British Columbia. America's preoccupation with the Civil War in the early 1860s had cooled such ambitions, but that conflict ended in 1865. Left with a vast and suddenly idle army, Americans began to rebuild their shattered nation, and some looked to the northwest and again thought about expansion. In a country that believed its manifest destiny was to dominate the continent, such territorial ambitions were well received in many quarters. Macdonald's smile faded as he remembered the successful wars the United States fought with Mexico over Texas and California and its triumph in the dispute with Great Britain over the Oregon Territory. It was quite possible that the United States might find Rupert's Land inviting.

Macdonald turned from the map and walked to his desk where a tumbler of gin rested. He lifted the glass to his mouth and swallowed. He moved to the window, and as he looked upon the Rideau Canal, he contemplated the task of populating the West, which he considered necessary to dull American interest in the region. Macdonald did not anticipate difficulties in attracting settlers. He had only to consider the U.S. to see how anxious immigrants were for an opportunity to homestead. Its western population had multiplied many times in the past few decades. Macdonald was confident that a similar pattern would emerge in Canada's West. But confidence gave way to concern as Macdonald recalled the price of America's western expansion. It was a bloody affair, accompanied by costly Native warfare.

Like many North Americans, Macdonald had read the newspapers that described the violence of the American frontier. In 1862, the Santee Sioux in Minnesota killed 800 settlers and soldiers. In 1865 the Oglala Sioux in and around Montana Territory had forced the United States government to retreat, abandoning several of its forts. Macdonald closed his eyes and

rubbed his forehead as he recalled other episodes of such warfare with the Apache and Comanche in the south. He rubbed
harder as he imagined Rupert's Land stained red with blood,
an outcome that would prove disastrous for the Dominion.
Macdonald was aware that in recent years the United States'
annual expenditure in fighting the Plains Natives was the
equivalent to Canada's annual revenue. Such an expense would
bankrupt the nascent Dominion.

Violence would bring additional problems. It would deter
settlers, undermining the West's economic value to Canada.
Furthermore, it might prove encouraging to American expan-
sionists. The United States government was so determined to
subdue Natives that it might be inclined to send troops into
Rupert's Land to address any violence there. Macdonald feared
that such troops would not be easily removed.

Determined that violence not accompany the settlement
of the Canadian West, Macdonald had given careful consideration to how Natives and settlers might live there peace-
fully. Military action was out of the question. It was too costly
and, if the American example was any indication, of dubi-
ous value. But Canada had a tradition of respectful relations
with its Native peoples. Historically, the British government
had recognized that North American Natives owned the land
they lived upon, and for the most part, the territory that
became Canada had been acquired by treaty with the Natives.
Macdonald believed that making treaty remained the appropriate strategy to extinguish Native rights in the West as well.
But how could western Natives be so convinced? And how
would law and order be maintained before the treaties were
made and, subsequently, while eastern immigrants established their settlements?

Macdonald thought the solution lay in a military-style
police force, a corps of mounted riflemen able to respond
quickly to disputes anywhere in the West. The Royal Irish

Constabulary offered a desirable model. The force had developed against a backdrop of sectarian violence and civil strife of early 19th-century Ireland, and it had been successfully deployed in other British colonies with large native populations. The force had earned the respect of local communities by recruiting members from those communities and by enforcing the law rather than serving the whims of local authorities. Macdonald wanted the force to be controlled by the Dominion government and to act in place of any corrupt or self-interested local law enforcement. He believed that such a structure would reduce much of the lawlessness characteristic of the American West, which he attributed to the absence of a centrally controlled police force.

The most significant community in Rupert's Land was Red River, which sprawled along the Red and Assiniboine Rivers in the southeastern corner of the territory. Lord Selkirk had created the settlement as a refuge for Scottish immigrants in the early 1800s. Since then it had attracted retired HBC employees and British and French Métis, the mixed-blood offspring of fur traders and Natives. According to the model of the Royal Irish Constabulary, Red River's population necessitated that half of the force be Métis. Macdonald planned that the local military garrison of Fort Garry would serve as the seat for the colonial government and as the headquarters of the Dominion police force.

Macdonald chose Captain Donald Cameron to lead the force, tentatively called the Mounted Rifles. He was the son-in-law of the important Nova Scotian politician Charles Tupper, and an officer in the Royal Artillery; he clearly possessed the proper political and military credentials. Already he was escorting the lieutenant-governor to Fort Garry. Once the transfer of Rupert's Land was complete and the lieutenant-governor was in control, Cameron would begin the business of creating the police force.

Macdonald sat down, picked up his quill, dipped it in ink and began a letter to Cameron, reminding him of the important details of the police force:

> *I have no doubt that, come what may, there must be a military body, or, at all events, a body with military discipline at Fort Garry. It seems to me the best Force would be Mounted Riflemen trained first as cavalry, but also instructed in the rifle exercises. They should be instructed in the use of artillery and should be styled Police and have the military bearing of the Irish Constabulary.*

When the prime minister finished the letter, the smile returned to his face. It seemed a simple matter of waiting for the British Crown to transfer ownership of Rupert's Land to the Dominion. The Canadian empire lay on the horizon.

But dark clouds unexpectedly clouded that horizon at Red River. Led by the Métis Louis Riel, most settlers in that region rebelled against the plan to establish a colonial government there. They were opposed to a future dictated by a distant Dominion government, which they anticipated would be insensitive to their concerns. Instead, they demanded to join Canada as a province and took up arms to emphasize their position. Events unfolded throughout the fall and winter of 1869–70. The lieutenant-governor and his entourage, including Cameron, were refused entry into the settlement when they arrived at the end of October. In late November, the Red River community elected a provisional government that created a list of rights, including self-government and guarantees of bilingualism, which it held as the basis for negotiating terms of Confederation with the Dominion government.

Macdonald seethed as he read the reports outlining the events. He was eager to counter the insurrection because it delayed the transfer of Rupert's Land to the Dominion, but political divisions in Canada made any action difficult. Québec politicians and electors who shared the French and Catholic heritage of the Métis and were sensitive to their demands for self-rule and cultural protection supported the Métis cause. And many in English Protestant Ontario were just as vocal that Métis demands be met with armed troops and that their leaders be punished. Fortunately for Macdonald, his choice was made for him. No accessible winter route to transfer troops to Red River forced the prime minister to negotiate. In March, a delegation from Red River arrived in Ottawa to negotiate the matter, and the result was the province of Manitoba, as recognized by the Manitoba Act of May 1870.

The events in Red River emphasized the need for law and order in Rupert's Land. In the spring, Macdonald considered instructing Cameron to forge ahead with the creation of a force of mounted riflemen. Given the Métis' actions, however, it seemed hardly likely that they would join such a force. More importantly, Macdonald no longer trusted them to police the region. Nevertheless, he was under pressure to act. Opponents to negotiation remained upset with the prime minister's course of action, and he had to appease them. So, in the spring, he dispatched the Red River Expedition, under the command of Colonel Garnet Wolseley. The military undertaking consisted of the 60th Rifle Battalion and two militia battalions. For the time being, Wolseley was responsible for maintaining the peace in Red River.

On July 15 1870, a day heavy with humidity, Macdonald sat at his desk, occasionally wiping his forehead with a handkerchief and reading an official dispatch from London. It informed him that Rupert's Land, renamed the North-West Territories, was officially transferred to Canada. Macdonald let slip a humorless chuckle and lifted a tumbler of gin to his mouth. Once he imagined he'd use it to toast the news. Today it served only to console him. The transfer was made official on

The Red River Expedition, depicted here in F.A. Hopkins' painting *Red River Expedition* (1870), was a 1200-man force of British soldiers and Canadian militia sent by the Dominion government to Manitoba in the late spring of 1870 to maintain order after the Red River Rebellion. Many Métis were concerned about the expedition's intent, despite commander Colonel Garnet Wolseley's public proclamations that the expedition's mission was peaceful. Their worries were well founded; Wolseley revealed privately his intention to punish rebel leaders. Wolseley departed Red River in September, but two battalions of militia remained to garrison the settlement. Their presence allowed Prime Minister Macdonald to delay the creation and deployment of the NWMP. Several members of the force who marched west in 1874 were veterans of the Red River Expedition, including James Macleod and Sam Steele.

the same day that the Manitoba Act received Royal Assent, and
Manitoba joined the Dominion as its fifth province.

Macdonald stood and walked to the map on his wall. The
new province wasn't much in size, only 13,500 square miles
and dwarfed by the North-West Territories, which was about
10 times the size of Canada. But its size gave no indication of
its disruptive effect on Macdonald's vision for the West. The
force of mounted riflemen he had once deemed necessary to
lay a foundation for law and order in the vast territory no
longer seemed practical. His reasons were two-fold. The British
North America Act, the legislation that created Canada, designated law enforcement as a provincial responsibility. A police
force under Dominion control could not be stationed in Manitoba. It could, of course, be located in the North-West Territories,
but Macdonald saw that the immediate issue was maintaining
law and order in Manitoba, and Wolseley's force was charged
with that responsibility. The prime minister was not inclined to
spend more of the Dominion's limited resources on policing
the West, despite his hope for settlement there. Frugality dictated he shelve the plans for the mounted police force and perhaps delay the emergence of the Canadian empire.

Prime Minister John A. Macdonald laughed heartily, briefly
forgetting the stifling heat of the summer day in 1870. He had
just finished reading a testy letter from Hamilton Fish, the
United States Secretary of State. Evidently, the Americans were
none too pleased about the activities of "Canadian" Blackfoot
in Montana Territory.

Fish alleged that the Blackfoot were crossing into American
territory to steal horses and murder settlers. Furthermore, when
the Blackfoot returned to Canada, they sold the stolen horses
for rifles, ammunition and whiskey, which further fueled their
southern aggression. The allegation had initially elicited a frown

from Macdonald because he knew the HBC did not trade alcohol to the Natives and had not engaged in that illegal practice for many years. Surely Fish was the victim of faulty intelligence.

But as Macdonald read on he realized he was mistaken. Fish was not suggesting that the HBC was the source of the whiskey. Rather it was American traders who could not sell alcohol to Natives in the U.S. Eager to be law-abiding citizens, they instead traveled to Dominion territory with their wares because they knew such trade could occur there without interference.

"The situation," concluded Fish, "is intolerable."

Law-abiding whiskey traders! Intolerable! When Macdonald finished chuckling, he again scanned the letter in disbelief. While the prime minister might concede the Dominion government did not—and could not, given the expense— enforce the law in the North-West Territories, he hardly considered Fish's complaint reasonable. But as he recalled recent newspaper reports from the eastern United States, he realized that reason was irrelevant. The reports affirmed the atrocities noted by Fish. Macdonald had no way of knowing whether they were accurate, but he was doubtful. Nevertheless, even if the reports were exaggerated they did cause a problem. If the United States government was concerned about the activities of Natives in Canada, they might well use it as an excuse to send troops into the region, troops that were likely to stay.

Macdonald's good humor gave way to a headache, but he remained unwilling to send out either the military or the police at the whim of Canada's southern neighbor. Perhaps, however, it was time to gather some reliable information on activities in the far west. He sent a message to Adams Archibald, the lieutenant-governor of Manitoba and the North-West Territories, on the matter. Adams reported that HBC officials described a reign of chaos in the region. They claimed that the safety of company traders and the small settlements was at risk because of the American whiskey traders' irresponsible actions. They traded booze illegally to the Natives for their furs, and the Natives, either drunk or anxious to get more alcohol, threatened property and lives. With Macdonald's agreement, Archibald commissioned Lieutenant William F. Butler to travel west and determine the accuracy of the allegations. Specifically, Butler was instructed to "report upon the whole question of the existing state of affairs in that territory [the Saskatchewan Valley], and to state [his] views on what may be necessary to be done in the interest of peace and order."

In late March 1871, Macdonald received Butler's report. The lieutenant had traveled an impressive 2700 miles in 119 days. As the prime minister read the report, troubling sections attracted his attention.

> *The institutions of Law and Order, as understood in civilized communities, are wholly unknown in the regions of the Saskatchewan, insomuch as the country is without any executive organization, and destitute of any means to enforce the authority of law.*
>
> *I do not mean to assert that crime and outrage are of habitual occurrence among the people of this territory, or that a state of anarchy exists in any particular portion of it, but it is an undoubted fact that crimes of the most serious nature have been committed, in various places, by persons of mixed and native blood, without any vindication of the law being possible, and that the position of affairs rests at the present moment not on the just power of an executive to enforce obedience, but rather on the passive acquiescence of the majority of a scant population…the elements of disorder in the whole territory of Saskatchewan are for many causes, yearly on the rise.*

Macdonald noted Butler's observations on the reasons for the growing Native discontent. Settlers were killing off the buffalo, animals on which the Natives depended, and in some quarters, destitution was emerging as a concern. Settlers also used poison to kill wolves, which also killed Native dogs and horses. Natives blamed settlers for the introduction of small-pox that had decimated bands and tribes. Butler heaped particular scorn on the effects of American practices. The United States government's "war of extermination" against its own Native population was being fought uncomfortably close to the border and inflaming passions to the north. And American traders were a disruptive influence. Not only did they use alcohol to obtain furs, a practice long forbidden in the North-West Territories, but they actively sought to turn the Natives against the HBC by suggesting that company traders had cheated them.

As Macdonald read Butler's estimates on the number of Natives—about 18,000, including 2000 Métis—he was well aware that such populations could create significant barriers to peace in the North-West Territories. Especially troublesome were Butler's observations on the hostile relationship between the Blackfoot and Cree. As traditional enemies, bloodshed appeared inevitable whenever they met. Butler considered the conflict a significant problem, particularly given that the Cree, who traded more, were often found around the trading posts. When the Blackfoot occasionally came in to trade, the inevitable violence between the two tribes threatened traders and settlers.

Macdonald paused and recalled reports of an especially violent Native encounter in the autumn of 1870. Some 700 Cree and Assiniboine had attacked the Blackfoot near Fort Whoop-Up, an American whiskey traders' post near the junction of the St. Mary's and Old Man's Rivers. The Blackfoot launched a counterattack that left as many as 300 Cree and 40 Blackfoot dead. Eyewitnesses claimed that the river ran red with blood as the current swept bodies away. Clearly Butler was not under-estimating the animosity between the tribes.

Macdonald continued on to Butler's recommendations, and they caused him to recall his own plans for a force of mounted riflemen. Butler advised the Dominion government to create a force of up to 150 men to serve in the Saskatchewan valley. Ideally, one third would be mounted.

Macdonald reflected on Butler's report. As yet, few settlers had migrated to the North-West Territories, and he was not inclined to spend more Dominion resources to provide law enforcement for the HBC. The militia at Fort Garry would have to suffice for now, and action on Butler's recommendation for a "well-equipped force" would not be forthcoming. Nevertheless, Old Tomorrow, as the prime minister was known for his procrastinating ways, realized it was necessary to do something. Those in the West voiced a growing criticism of the Dominion government's policy in the North-West Territories. While Macdonald might brush aside the self-serving braying of Hudson's Bay Company officials, reports from missionaries active in the region were more troubling. They demanded action to deal with the American whiskey traders whose activities disrupted Native communities.

Macdonald, eager to save money under the guise of promoting law and order, decided to address the matter through a crafty act of political delay. The Dominion government dispatched Colonel Patrick Robertson-Ross on yet another fact-finding mission to the North-West Territories. Robertson-Ross left Fort Garry on August 10, 1872, and by mid-December, he was back in Ottawa to report directly to the prime minister. The colonel joined Macdonald in his office.

"I'm pleased to report that our party met with no significant difficulties, Mr. Prime Minister," said Robertson-Ross.

"I'm glad to hear it," replied Macdonald. "You traveled all the way to the Pacific Ocean?"

"We did, by way of the North Saskatchewan River and the North Kootenay Pass."

"And what of the reports that the country is without law and order?"

"I'd have to agree. As of late, no attempt has been made to assert the supremacy of law, and serious crimes go unpunished. For example, at Fort Edmonton there is a notorious murderer, a Cree Indian, Tahakooch, who has committed several murders and who should have been apprehended long ago. The man walks openly about the post. Many instances can be adduced of a similar kind," added Robertson-Ross, "and as a natural result there is a widespread feeling of apprehension."

"Apprehension?"

"Yes. Let me elaborate. The gentleman in charge of the HBC Post at Fort Pitt, as well as others elsewhere, assured me that of late the Indians have been overbearing in manner and threatening at times. The traders fear that without a military force, even more serious trouble can be anticipated."

"Yes, the HBC is anxious to have its interests protected," observed Macdonald.

"It's not only the HBC, sir. The white men living in the Saskatchewan are at this moment living by sufferance, as it were, entirely at the mercy of the Indians. They dare not introduce cattle or stock into the country or cultivate the land to any extent for fear of Indian plunder. And there is the ever-present and great danger of being mistaken for an American citizen while approaching the international line near the Porcupine Hills. One could meet with hostile bands of Gros Ventres and Crow Indians from Dakota and Montana territories, who frequently cross into Dominion territory on horse-stealing expeditions. Such Indians are not likely, if they fall in with travelers, to make distinctions."

"And the American whiskey traders I've heard so much of?"

"When I was at Fort Edmonton and Rocky Mountain House, I was informed that a party of American smugglers and traders established a trading post at the junction of the Bow and Belly

Rivers, about 30 miles due east of the Porcupine Hills, and about 60 miles on the Dominion side of the boundary line. They named it Fort Hamilton, after the mercantile firm of Hamilton, Healy and Company of Fort Benton, Montana, from whom it is said they obtain supplies. It is believed that they number about 20 well-armed men under the command of John Healy, a notorious character.

"It appears that for some time they have carried on an extensive trade with the Blackfoot Indians, supplying them with rifles, revolvers, whiskey and other ardent spirits, in direct opposition to the laws both of the United States and the Dominion of Canada, and without paying any customs duties for the goods introduced into Canada."

Macdonald nodded. Robertson-Ross' observations confirmed some of the American secretary of state's allegations.

"Their brazenness is limitless," continued Robertson-Ross. "At Fort Edmonton this past summer, whiskey was openly sold to the Blackfoot and other Indians trading at the post by smugglers from the United States who derive large profits. And when the gentleman in charge of the Hudson's Bay Company post remonstrated the smugglers, they coolly replied that they knew very well that their actions were illegal in both countries, but with no force there to prevent them, they would do just as they pleased.

"The demoralization of the Indians, danger to the white inhabitants and injury resulting to the country from this illicit traffic is very great," said Robertson-Ross.

"Great yes, but yet manifested?" asked Macdonald.

"I have it on good authority that during the year 1871, 88 Blackfeet Indians were murdered in drunken brawls amongst themselves, produced by whiskey and other spirits supplied by those traders." He paused, then continued. "Year after year, these unscrupulous traders continue to plunder our Indians of their buffalo robes and valuable furs by extortion and fraud, and the shameful traffic causes certain bloodshed amongst the Indian tribes.

"It is indispensable for the peace of the country and welfare of the Indians that this smuggling and illicit trade in spirits and firearms be stopped. A custom house with a military guard near the Porcupine Hills would stop this traffic, and it would also stop the horse-stealing expeditions carried on by hostile Indians from the south of the line into Dominion Territory—that's the real cause of all danger in that part of the country and the source of constant war among the Indian tribes. Indeed, to stop horse stealing and selling spirits to Indians is to stop altogether the Indian wars in the North West.

"Any additional recommendations on a military presence, colonel?" asked Macdonald.

Robertson-Ross clasped his hands behind his back and paced the floor in front of Macdonald's desk, "My recommendations are based on an estimate of between 14,000 and 15,000 prairie Indians, scattered over an immense extent of country. Bear in mind too, that in addition to the Indian element, there is a Half-breed population of about 2000 souls in the Saskatchewan valley, unaccustomed to the restraint of any government, mainly depending upon the chase for subsistence and needing control nearly as much as the Indians." He studied the tips of his boots for a moment.

"No doubt whatever exists in my mind of the necessity for maintaining any military force at Fort Garry. I feel satisfied that the preservation of good order and peace in the North-West Territories, under the changing state of affairs will, for some years, lie in the presence of a disciplined military body, under its own military rules, in addition to, but distinct from, any civil force which it may be thought proper to establish."

He continued with his recommendation, "One regiment of mounted riflemen, 550 strong, that includes non-commissioned officers divided into companies of 50 would be a sufficient force to support the government in establishing law and order in the Saskatchewan valley and preserving the peace of the North-West Territories. My report includes proposed locations for their deployment." He eased back into his chair.

"I should add, Mr. Prime Minister, that it is advantageous they be dressed in red. During my inspection in the North-West I ascertained that some prejudice existed amongst the Indians against the color of the uniform worn by the U.S. military. Many of them said 'who are those soldiers at Red River wearing dark clothes? Our old brothers who formerly lived there—meaning H.M.S. 6th Regiment—wore red coats. We know that the soldiers of our great mother wear red coats and are our friends.' British scarlet would surely gain the respect of the Indians as nothing else would."

Macdonald thanked Robertson-Ross for his service to the Dominion and dismissed him. The evidence was mounting that law enforcement was necessary in the North-West Territories. Still, Macdonald was not convinced that the need was urgent, especially given the costs involved. Earlier in the month, Alexander Morris had been appointed the new lieutenant-governor of Manitoba and the North-West Territories. Macdonald decided action on law enforcement could wait until Morris offered his observations on the matter.

Prime Minister John A. Macdonald strolled through the parliamentary grounds. The first blossoms of spring 1873 should have put him in a positive frame of mind, but he thought of Lieutenant-Governor Alexander Morris and heaved yet another sigh of despair. While Morris undoubtedly shared his optimism regarding the Dominion's bright future and the critical role of the North-West Territories in that future, he had a most distressing way of showing it. Since his appointment in December 1872, Morris had deluged Macdonald with letters

Alexander Morris (1826–89), lieutenant-governor of Manitoba and the North-West Territories, who accelerated the creation of the NWMP

~⚹~

detailing the disaster that would ensue unless the Dominion government act immediately to address Native unrest. Morris' missives were so dark and pessimistic that Macdonald considered him an alarmist who surely exaggerated the situation in the North-West Territories.

In one letter Macdonald received from Morris in January, Morris argued that a military and a police force would be necessary if a disaster like that of Minnesota in 1862 was to be avoided. Macdonald mused that if Morris believed that the Dominion government could afford the upkeep of both a military *and* a police force in the North-West Territories, he was sadly misinformed about the country's resources. Moreover, the Santee Sioux outbreak in Minnesota had occurred more than a decade earlier, and it hardly seemed appropriate for use as illustration of what could happen in the Canadian West. But Macdonald couldn't dispute the mounting evidence in support of law enforcement west of Manitoba. The reports of Butler, Robertson-Ross, HBC officials, missionaries and Morris all pointed to the danger of inaction.

Macdonald's view of the North-West Territories had not changed substantially since 1869. He continued to envision the region filled with settlers, and to that end, his government had passed the Dominion Lands Act in 1872. But the free land the legislation promised had not yet attracted many settlers west, and Macdonald no longer considered settlement an immediate prospect. The situation surrounding the North-West Territories had changed in other ways during the past few years. In 1871, the United States and Britain signed the Treaty of Washington, confirming the borders between the United States and Canada. While problems with American whiskey traders and their destructive influence on the Natives remained, the threat of American expansion into Canada was reduced substantially. In the same year, British Columbia entered the Dominion. The colony's demands for joining Confederation included the construction of a transcontinental railroad. To guarantee the right of way for construction, access through Native land was necessary. Furthermore, to ensure the safety of the railway's work crews, the Natives would have to be kept peaceful.

Increasingly, Macdonald realized that the dangers and threats to his vision for the North-West Territories were all linked to western Natives. Peace in the West demanded pacified Natives.

Macdonald continued to believe that peace could best be achieved through treaty, which protected Native rights and recognized Canadian needs. Therefore, it was essential to lay a foundation for treaty making. To do that, Native confidence had to be gained.

Aware that he had to address the situation, Macdonald headed for the House of Commons, where he announced the proposed bill "Respecting the Administration of Justice and for the Establishment of a Police Force in the North-West Territories." Perhaps his critics would be surprised that Old Tomorrow had finally made a decision.

Macdonald was pleased, but hardly surprised, that debate on the topic was insignificant. The most meaningful alteration to the proposed legislation came about not as a result of parliamentary debate or public pressure. The impetus for change wasn't even Canadian. The bill referred to the proposed police force as the "Mounted Rifles," which unsettled the Americans. They were alarmed at the possibility of an armed military force patrolling their northern boundary. Hackles of red, white and blue rose high in indignation. Anxious to silence the unpleasant squawking, he defused the situation with a simple stroke of his pen. Gone was "Mounted Rifles," and in its place was written "Mounted Police." It was a small sacrifice, since Macdonald saw the force as primarily a civilian body.* And perhaps the gesture would be sufficient to dull American interest in that enterprise.

On May 23, 1873, the act that outlined the organization, administration and duties of the mounted police force for the North-West Territories received Royal Assent. The act

---

*It was not until 1879, when the Act was amended, that the mounted police force was officially titled the North-West Mounted Police, however, that was its popular name, and its members were called Mounties.

established the framework for the force. The Department of Justice (of which Macdonald was minister) was placed in control of the force. Its internal hierarchy consisted of a supervising commissioner under whom served superintendents for each of the force's divisions.* These officers were also justices of the peace. The bulk of the force consisted of constables and sub-constables, who were given the rights to detain and arrest suspects. Recruits, not to exceed 300 in number, had to be of sound constitution, active and able-bodied, able to ride and be of good character. They also had to be between 18 and 40 and be literate in either English or French. The duties and domain of the force were widely cast, and they demanded extensive powers to ensure success. Generally, the force's mandate was to preserve peace, prevent crime and apprehend criminals throughout the North-West Territories. More specifically, Macdonald wanted the force to address the problems associated with the Natives: stop the illegal liquor trade, earn their respect and confidence, teach them to obey the law and prepare them for the changes—including treaty—that would inevitably transform their world.

For their efforts, members of the Mounted Police received payment based on a graduated scale. The commissioner would be paid up to $2600 and superintendents up to $1400 annually. Constables and sub-constables would receive a daily rate

---

*While Macdonald envisioned the North-West Mounted Police to be a civilian body, he anticipated that many of its members would come from the military. Thus, the act identified the military equivalents of the officers' ranks: commissioner/lieutenant colonel; and superintendent (later inspectors)/captain. Many, but not all, officers would continue to be referred to by their military rank even if it did not correspond to the appropriate rank within the North-West Mounted Police.

of up to $1 and $.75 respectively. The Dominion government would supply necessities, including uniforms, horses and rations. In addition, constables and sub-constables who satis-factorily performed their duties for a period of three years were eligible for a grant of 160 acres, as Butler suggested, in either Manitoba or the North-West Territories. The Dominion gov-ernment saw such men as a strong settler foundation on which to build western Canada.

The legislation of 1873 was, for the most part, a reflection of Macdonald's earlier plans. But although the force was modeled on the Royal Irish Constabulary and controlled by Dominion government, it deviated from Macdonald's original vision. Gone, for example, was the stated desire to recruit Métis. Mac-donald remained bitter towards the Métis since the Red River Rebellion. It would have been difficult politically to exclude them from the force, but the educational requirements ensured that most Métis could not participate.

The act did not actually create the mounted police force. It was enabling legislation; the force would come into existence when authorized by the Dominion government Cabinet with an order-in-council. Macdonald, ever focused on the finan-cial bottom line, did not envision an immediate order-in-council. He planned to maintain the Fort Garry militia at its current strength for possibly one more year. At that time, per-haps around the summer of 1874, he would reduce the num-ber of troops in the militia and authorize the creation of the North-West Mounted Police. But Macdonald felt confident that he had done enough to satisfy his critics and convince the public and potential immigrants that the Dominion govern-ment was acting to maintain law and order in the North-West Territories.

The prime minister's natural inclination to procrastinate was unduly influenced by matters not related to law and order in the West during the summer of 1873, when the Pacific

Scandal emerged as the dominant political issue. Prior to the August 1872 election, Macdonald and his Conservative Party had received more than $350,000 in campaign funds from businessman Sir Hugh Allan. After the election, Allan received the contract to build a transcontinental railroad to and through British Columbia. While Macdonald saw the relationship as political *quid pro quo*, his detractors smelled corruption. The Liberals, the Conservatives' parliamentary opposition, first broke the story in April 1873, but it was not until July that newspaper headlines trumpeted the news. Despite a campaign by the Conservatives and their supporters to paint the issue as the Pacific Slander, mounting pressure forced Macdonald to act. Early in August, the government struck a royal commission to investigate the allegations. Macdonald hoped the delay brought by an investigation might allow the issue to blow over, but he was none too sure.

The intrigue surrounding the Pacific Scandal relegated all other matters, including the formation of the Mounted Police force, to secondary importance. Macdonald assigned Alexander Campbell, Minister of the Interior, to deal with the continuing stream of letters from Lieutenant-Governor Morris. Morris insisted that the whiskey traders were a greater problem than ever and the Blackfoot were a step away from the warpath. He demanded the force be sent without delay. Macdonald continued to believe that Morris overstated the case and instructed Campbell to inform him that circumstances in the West did not yet justify hastening the government's plans for the force's creation and deployment.

The reports Macdonald found on his desk in late summer suddenly changed that. In May, a band of Assiniboine was massacred in the Cypress Hills, less than 100 miles west of Fort Whoop-Up. It had taken the better part of the summer for the story to travel east, and details were sketchy. Apparently American wolfers had ridden from Fort Benton in search of horse thieves. They arrived at Fort Farwell, one of several trading posts in the region, where they found an Assiniboine camp. Fueled by alcohol, the Americans attacked the Natives, who by all accounts, were just as drunk. They assaulted Native women and killed approximately 30 Assiniboine, and as a final injustice, mutilated some of their bodies.

Macdonald required no more letters predicting disaster from Morris. On August 27, 1873, he recommended to Cabinet that a police force for the North-West Territories be constituted in accordance with the May legislation. Three hundred men in red uniforms, according to Robertson-Ross' recommendation, were to be divided into six divisions, lettered A to F, each with a superintendent (or inspector) and two sub-inspectors (lieutenants). Delays were forgotten; the Mounted Police force was finally a reality.

CHAPTER TWO

Recruitment and Organization

THE DECISION TO INITIATE the organization of the Mounted Police force brought up a long-standing and critical problem: Who would be the commissioner of the new force? Prime Minister John A. Macdonald, after much deliberation, decided that a British officer, preferably one with both Canadian and Royal Irish Constabulary experience, was best suited to the position.

Macdonald had been scrutinizing candidates perhaps as early as 1871. Initially, he had considered Captain David Cameron, who was charged with organizing the ill-fated force of mounted riflemen at Red River in 1869. Cameron, however, had accepted Macdonald's 1872 nomination as Canadian Commissioner of the North American Boundary Commission, a joint United States-British plan to survey the international boundary between Lake of the Woods and the Rocky Mountains.

In the fall of 1872, Macdonald had approached Colonel J.C. McNeill, aid to then Governor General Lord Lisgar. In a letter offering McNeill the position, Macdonald noted that the task "involves the watching of the Frontier from Manitoba to the foot of the Rocky Mountains; and will have its civil side as well as military side, as the person in command will have to hold the position of Stipendiary or Police Magistrate." Whether McNeill was daunted by the immensity of the task, unenthusiastic about the civilian duties demanded of the force, or put off by the uncertainty that seemed to characterize the force itself, he rejected the offer and instead chose to join the British fighting in West Africa.

Although others were suggested or applied for the commissioner's position, no one met Macdonald's criteria. But with the force's organization underway, Macdonald turned to the governor general, the Earl of Dufferin, for assistance in September 1873. Macdonald hoped Dufferin could encourage the British government to lend the Dominion government an officer to lead the force. Given his difficulties in recruiting an appropriate man, Macdonald also sought to enhance the terms of appointment by requesting that if the British government agreed, the appointment be regarded as pensionable military service. Macdonald hoped it would be enough to persuade the right man.

About the same time, Macdonald also wrote Lieutenant-Governor Alexander Morris, to inform him of the Dominion government's decision to initiate the organization of the North-West Mounted Police. Macdonald anticipated one of his most vocal critics on North-West Territories policy would be silenced with the news that the force would be recruited in the fall, drilled in Toronto throughout the winter and deployed west in the spring. With satisfaction, he informed Morris that recruiters were already traveling throughout the four original provinces in search of recruits. The prime minister had confidence in the government's plan and assumed that Morris would share his opinion.

Unfortunately, the lieutenant-governor was not appeased and continued to insist that the Natives were on the verge of open warfare. Furthermore, Morris' new intelligence suggested that the Métis were active among the tribes, encouraging them to reject any treaty efforts by the Dominion government. Morris suspected that Louis Riel, in exile in the U.S., was somehow behind the effort, and he worried that the involvement of the Métis leader could mean trouble.

"The feeling of many Métis in the North-West is bad," wrote Morris. "There is undoubtedly danger that the scene of 1869 may be repeated in the North-West, but I believe it would be prevented by the presence of a [police] force."

Morris included an ominous warning that echoed in Macdonald's thoughts. "What you have done as to the police force, their absence may lead to grave disaster."

Given the difficulties associated with the yet unsettled Pacific Scandal, Macdonald needed no more "grave disasters." He decided to appease Morris by advancing the time line for the force. They would be sent to Lower Fort Garry in Manitoba, drill there over the winter and march west in the spring. But the changed plans presented a new problem. Recruits would have to travel by the Dawson Route, the only all-Canadian route linking Manitoba with Ontario. But the part-land, part-water route was not accessible after winter freeze-up, which usually occurred about mid-October. Haste was suddenly necessary.

Macdonald found his quill and began a letter to Governor General Dufferin to explain the change in plans.

"It would not be well for us to take the responsibility of slighting Morris' repeated and urgent entreaties. If anything went wrong, the blame would lie at our door. I shall hurry the men off at once. No time is to be lost."

The race to send the mounted police force west had begun.

On September 25, Prime Minister Macdonald sat in his office reading over the list of proposed officers for the Mounted Police force. Their proper selection was a matter of critical importance, and the prime minister wanted to review the names once more before the Cabinet meeting that would issue an order-in-council authorizing the appointments. On the list was Lieutenant Colonel W. Osbourne Smith, who was chosen to serve as temporary commissioner. Smith was the obvious, if not ideal, man to lead the force in its initial months of organization. As Deputy Adjutant General in military district No. 10, Manitoba, stationed at Fort Garry, Smith's primary responsibility was to ready the force's temporary headquarters at Lower Fort Garry for their arrival. He would prepare the barracks, contract for supplies and acquire horses and equipment. Macdonald anticipated that Smith could use his military position both to speed up preparations and ensure any additional logistical and financial support. He did not see Smith as the force's permanent commissioner, because his appointment would have tied the force more tightly to the military than Macdonald thought appropriate.

Charles Young, Ephrem Brisebois, William Winder, James Walsh, William Jarvis, James Macleod, Jacob Carvell, John Breden and Edmund Clark were on the list of selected officers, each to be paid an annual salary of $1000. Most had military experience in Canada, either in the regular forces or the militia. Again, Macdonald was aware that men drawn from the ranks of the military might undermine his desire to create a civilian force, but he was also sensitive to the critical role that the officers would play. The mission required men who could organize, command and ride with troops, and such men were found in the military.

But Macdonald also wanted officers of social standing, men who placed the good of the community above self-interest. The officers would be responsible for establishing the foundation for settlement and, subsequently, maintaining a peaceful and prosperous society in the North-West Territories. The weighty charge had to be accepted as a matter of duty, and Macdonald

James Macleod (1836–94) started his career with the NWMP as an inspector, became its first assistant commissioner and retired as its second commissioner.

believed that confident men of elevated class were best suited to the task. And, at an organizational level, Macdonald expected the officers to serve as models of appropriate behavior and deportment for the troopers.

Macdonald glanced again at the men's qualifications. Macleod was a lawyer with a university degree and had served as a brigade major with the Red River Expedition. Walsh was a hotel manager and had won honors at the Kingston School of Cavalry and the Militia School of Gunnery at Toronto. His command of the Prescott Cavalry Troop had won the praise of Governor General Dufferin. Jarvis had served with the 12th Foot Militia and was the nephew of Deputy Minister of Justice Hewitt Bernard, who was directly responsible for the Mounted Police force and a relative of Prime Minister Macdonald by marriage.

Macdonald didn't need to continue. He knew the accomplishments and standings of the men and had no doubt that they were up to the task. He left for the Cabinet meeting.

Less than two weeks later, in early October, Macdonald reviewed the recruiting reports of the officers. They had been busy enlisting troopers in Ontario, Québec, New Brunswick and Nova Scotia since their appointments, and Macdonald was pleased to note that they had met their quotas of 20–40 men each, despite certain obstacles. In Nova Scotia, the local press challenged Charles Young and questioned whether men likely to earn a good wage in the Maritimes should set out for the uncertainty of the North-West Territories. In Québec, Ephrem Brisebois faced the indignation of the English press when it learned that information regarding recruitment had appeared only in French newspapers.

Macdonald considered these and others to be minor complaints, made mostly in newspapers controlled by the Liberal party opposition. Even with minimal advertising, the officers interviewed more men than there were available positions in the force. More troublesome news was that appropriate selection procedures were necessarily undermined because transportation along the Dawson Route would be impossible after October 10 because of the weather. Despite the best efforts of the officers, orders to hastily select approximately 150 men meant that the finer points of a recruit's abilities and aptitudes were overlooked. Required references could not be checked, and alleged experiences could not be verified. Did a trooper have the desired character? Could he ride a horse or shoot a gun? Could he abide by the rules and live within the constraints of the force? Much would be taken at face value during these first few rushed weeks, but Macdonald wasn't overly concerned. A year in the North-West Territories would provide its own process of selection.

Macdonald noted the details of the recruits' backgrounds. The majority came from Ontario, drawn by a sense of adventure. Some were born in Britain, and they were perhaps eager to join a force with a rigid organizational structure akin to their own youthful experiences. While many of the recruits had military experience, they were not the traditional members of a military or policing force, drawn from the lower classes. Recruiting efforts were guided by the notion that the force was an elite organization for educated men from good families. The qualifications helped to weed out the uneducated. For the most part, those recruited as constables and sub-constables were members of the lower middle class; skilled workers, farmers and clerks filled the ranks.

The reports also indicated that the recruits had taken the oaths of allegiance and office:

> I, _____, solemnly swear that I will faithfully, diligently and impartially execute and perform the duties and offices of _____ in the Police Force of the North-West Territories, and will well and truly obey and perform all lawful orders or instructions which I shall receive as such _____, without fear, favor, or affection of or towards any person whomsoever. So help me God.

The reports concluded with notice that those officers with their recruitment quotas filled were en route to Collingwood, Ontario. On the southern shore of Georgian Bay,

Collingwood was the eastern terminus of the Dawson Route, where the force would assemble prior to their departure for Manitoba. In mid-September, Major D.A. McDonald had been appointed Movement Control Officer responsible for coordinating the force's arrival in Collingwood and ensuring successful transportation of all men and necessary equipment to Lower Fort Garry. He supplied each recruit with essential items, including a greatcoat, utensils, soap and towel, all of which came from militia stores. He also arranged for three Northern Railway Company steamers, the *Cumberland*, the *Chicora* and the *Frances Smith*, to ferry the men to Prince Arthur's Landing (present-day Thunder Bay) on the western shore of Lake Superior.

On October 10, a telegram reached the hands of Hewitt Bernard, and he hurried to the prime minister's office to share important news regarding the police force. He took an informal tone with his boss, who was also his father-in-law.

"Good news, John! The mounted police force has left Collingwood for the Stone Fort at Lower Fort Garry."

"You're certain?" asked Macdonald.

"We received a telegram from Major McDonald last night. The last of the recruits left on the *Frances Smith* yesterday evening."

"Ahh, good news indeed!" The prime minister rubbed his hands together.

"By God, it must have been a busy week at Collingwood," observed Hewitt.

"Undoubtedly," agreed Macdonald. "But more strenuous days await. I'll wager the men will soon recall their brief interlude at Collingwood with fondness."

Major James Walsh possessed a temper similar to a prairie thunderstorm. Under the right conditions, it broke unexpectedly, throwing those around him under the darkness of foul and critical language. In mid-October, he watched helplessly as his command of 31 men drifted on barges in the open cove of the North West Angle of Lake of the Woods and suffered the freezing wind and beating snow. The conditions were about right for that thunderstorm to break.

Walsh's temper had been simmering for some time, and it was a credit to his self-control that it hadn't yet exploded. Responsible for recruiting in eastern Ontario, Walsh had arrived in Collingwood with his men on October 1 and discovered that the transport steamer *Cumberland* was delayed and wouldn't arrive for another 24 hours. The men had turned to liquor to pass the time, and although he enjoyed a drink as much as the next man, Walsh warned his men that their behavior would justify the trust placed in them. Nevertheless, the next day he had to discharge one trooper because of a drunken disturbance. Walsh knew that the action didn't show much for his own ability to judge character, but the selection process had left little time for careful consideration. Mostly sober troopers boarded the *Cumberland* on October 4 and arrived at Prince Arthur's Landing on October 8, where the 545 miles of the Dawson Route awaited them.

Under the best conditions, the Dawson Route was a challenge, with waterways connected by nearly 50 portages of corduroy roads (muddy roads shored up with untrimmed logs as a surface). At both Lake Shebandowan and Island Portage, no steamers waited, thus causing additional unnecessary delays. By the time the troops reached Fort Frances, the HBC post on Rainy Lake, the weather had turned icy. As the steamer proceeded to the North West Angle, the next stop on the journey, sleet and harsh northerly winds added to the men's discomfort.

Sight of the port brought short-lived relief. The water around the North West Angle was too shallow for the steamer to make port, so the men were required to disembark onto barges

As a young man, the fiery James M. Walsh (1840–1905) struggled to find a suitable career before settling on the military. In his mid-twenties, he was commissioned a lieutenant and posted to the 156th Grenville Regiment. Walsh impressed his superiors with his ability to gain his men's respect and promoted him to captain. Walsh went on to gain honors at the Kingston School of Cavalry and the Toronto Militia School of Gunnery. He planned to join the Red River Expedition but instead married and stayed in Brockville with his wife Elizabeth, where he settled into the life of a businessman as the manager of a local hotel. Walsh remained active as the commander of the Prescott Cavalry Troop but pined for greater adventure. When he learned that the Dominion government was organizing the NWMP, he sought adventure there.

pulled ashore by a tug. The tug made it to shore easily enough, but it let the barges drift. Only when the wind and the waves grounded the vessels were the men able to disembark. A seething Walsh made his way to George Dixon, the engineer of the tug.

"Goddammit man! What the hell was that about?" he roared, teeth flashing between a sharply trimmed moustache and goatee. "I had sick men aboard those barges. Cripes, even the healthy ones were at risk of exposure!"

"Now listen—"

"Listen nothing! You're a goddamn black-hearted villain, one step away from being a murderer! Leaving us out there in this kind of weather!"

"I don't have to take—," sputtered Dixon.

"You'll take what I give you, and a hell of a lot more if I had my way," interrupted Walsh. "Where I come from, we'd shoot a man like you and not give it a second thought!"

Walsh berated the engineer for the better part of half an hour with colorful barrage of barrack's language, until the brow-beaten Dixon managed to escape.

Many men heard Walsh's castigation of the engineer, while others heard about it later that night. Most made mental notes to avoid the major's bad side, but the episode gave them more confidence in the 33-year-old officer. He was clearly a man who stood for no nonsense, quick to act and stand up for his men. Troopers would follow a man like that. For his part, Walsh gave thanks that the remainder of the journey to Lower Fort Garry would be on foot or by wagon.

Major James Macleod also looked forward to the land journey of the Dawson Route. His men, among the last group of recruits to leave Collingwood, endured a hellish crossing on Lake Superior. The *Frances Smith* had been tossed on the lake's great gray waves like a ball in a child's hands. The captain had chuckled as he claimed that it was the fiercest storm he'd seen in years. While the pronouncement did little to raise spirits, Macleod believed it. Only hours after leaving port on October 10, the recruits' faces mirrored the lake's ashen gray pallor. But Macleod was determined that the elements would not best him. It was more than a natural inclination that demanded he remain strong; he was resolved to show the men the fortitude they would need on their mission. Those troopers who had the energy to go topside to dispose of what little food they forced down marveled at his presence at the bow of the steamer, his unusually long, full sideburns pinned by the wind. Lake Superior threw him her worst, and it had all the impact of a raindrop on granite.

More than a few smiles broke through when Prince Arthur's Landing came into sight a few days later. The 50-mile trek to Shebandowan was eased with the knowledge that each step took the troopers farther from Superior's wrath. But as they journeyed from Shebandowan to Fort Frances, the temperature plummeted, and snow began to fall. Enthusiasm sagged further with rumors that supplies were running low. Fortunately, the popular trading trail was dotted with stopping houses, which were mostly boarded up for the winter. Macleod didn't object when the troopers broke into and raided the establishments. Empty stomachs stopped grumbling, but only when the troopers finally reached Rainy River, and a band of friendly Chippewa treated them to a meal of boiled corn and whitefish, were they filled.

Although few would have realized it given his calm demeanor, Macleod shared the men's anger when they realized that the steamer hired to ferry them across the Lake of the Woods had not yet arrived and wouldn't for three days. Winter's grip was tight when the men finally boarded the vessel, and they gave thanks that the passage was a calm one. Soon enough, however, words of gratitude became streaks of profanity. When the steamer approached the landing point of North West Angle on October 24, they found the cove ice-locked. The men had to disembark the steamer and board barges towed ashore by a tugboat, but the small vessel did not have enough power to break the ice. Macleod quickly surveyed the situation and barked an order.

"Sergeant Major Bray, obtain whatever picks, axes and shovels you can and get the men over the side to chop us an opening to shore."

The men followed the order crisply, and when they were finally on land they were cold and wet when the blizzard came.

"We can't unpack the tents, sir," Bray informed Macleod. "They got wet aboard the steamer, and they're frozen stiff."

"They're what?" shouted Macleod. Bray's words were lost in the howling wind.

"Frozen stiff," he called, grabbing the ropes on one of the tent bags to demonstrate its stiffness.

Through the thick blowing snow, Macleod could just make out Bray. He stepped towards him and placed his hand on the bag. Immediately he knew that it would be impossible to unpack the tents.

"Have the men build some bivouacs," directed Macleod. They'd offer little shelter, but it was better than nothing, and would keep the men active.

Early the next day, Macleod ordered the stiff and sleep-deprived men to prepare for the final march to Lower Fort Garry. Enthusiasm waned. The temperature had fallen below 0° F when the men turned their attention to the trail ahead. A quick reconnaissance revealed it deep with snow and interspersed with occasional patches of icy mud. No trooper was prepared for winter travel. Improvising, they wrapped whatever spare material they could find around their boots and legs. The journey was difficult, and Macleod soon gave the order to abandon many of the cumbersome supplies and equipment. As the major looked at his men and saw the broken trail of cargo behind them, his thoughts turned suddenly to history and Napoleon's march towards Moscow. He had a new compassion for the lot of the French soldiers. When he recalled the disaster that accompanied that expedition, he pushed such thoughts from his mind.

While the men toiled along the Dawson Route, the Dominion government issued an order-in-council appointing George A. French, captain in the Royal Artillery, Commissioner of the North-West Mounted Police. With the announcement, Prime Minister Macdonald was greatly relieved.

In many ways, the 32-year-old French was an ideal appointee because he met many qualifications Macdonald believed necessary for the position. He was born in Ireland and served briefly with the Royal Irish Constabulary. He was a veteran of the Maori War in New Zealand, and in 1871, he was seconded to Canada with the acting rank of lieutenant-colonel for the purpose of establishing and commanding the Canadian Militia gunnery school (the School of Artillery) at Kingston, Ontario. Macdonald received permission from the British Secretary of State for War to allow French to hold the appointment of commissioner while retaining his position on the Seconded List of the Royal Artillery. He thought it had been an important inducement, likely brought about by Governor General Dufferin's efforts.

Despite French's impressive list of accomplishments, he had his limitations. He was relatively young and had been a junior captain in the Royal Artillery for only a year prior to his commission with the Mounted Police. As a junior captain, his service was with garrison artillery, and he had little operational experience of value in the North-West Territories. Macdonald knew that French's inexperience troubled some, including Lieutenant-Governor Morris, but the prime minister believed it to be a trifling matter. In his opinion, French was qualified; the force had its permanent commissioner.

George A. French (1841–1921), first commissioner of the NWMP, whose leadership during the Mounties' march west was not without controversy

French was not present to greet the three contingents of troopers when they arrived at Lower Fort Garry, the headquarters of the North-West Mounted Police throughout the winter and spring of 1873–74. He did not actually take up his commission until mid-December. But French could not have done a better job preparing for the force's arrival than Acting Commissioner Osborne Smith. He negotiated with the HBC to secure quarters for the force in the Stone Fort, the historic administrative center for the company's operations in Rupert's Land. The Big House, once used by HBC governor George Simpson, was set aside for officers, while carpenters repaired and remodeled the barracks as necessary. The results were spartan and incomplete, but with large rooms bunking 12 men each, a certain degree of comfort existed. Smith also contracted the HBC to provide food for the troops. It was a most profitable relationship for the company and an invaluable one for the force.

The troops faced fewer physical tasks thanks to Smith's foresight in contracting convicts from the local penitentiary to move supplies. Smith turned to the local community for horses because he felt that eastern-bred horses would take too long to acclimatize to western conditions. He had acquired 33, too few for the entire force but enough for training purposes. The acting commissioner also used his connections with the military to secure enough rifles for proper training. And when the force's uniforms failed to arrive (likely left somewhere along the Dawson Route), Smith procured fatigue uniforms from local militia stores.

On November 3, with his work satisfactorily completed, Smith made the short 20-mile journey from Fort Garry to Lower Fort Garry to oversee a more pleasant task—a small ceremony in which each trooper signed his name on the articles of engagement and received his warrant of enlistment. The engagement oath pledged each man to uphold the directives of the "Act respecting the Administration of Justice, and for the Establishment of a Police Force in the North-West Territories." A simple enough request, it was met with unexpected confusion and protest as a handful of men argued that they were told that they could resign from the force at any time with six months notice. The act, however, stipulated that six months notice could be given only after three years of service. Smith determined that the misunderstanding was a result of poor communication lines during the period of hurried enlistment. The misinformed men were permitted to resign. Given local conditions, they were also allowed to remain until the spring and provided food for the duration.

The remaining men pledged that thoroughness, diligence, faithfulness and impartiality would characterize their service. After signing the articles of engagement, each man was given a warrant bearing his name and rank. This frosty November day truly marked the beginning of the North-West Mounted Police.

CHAPTER THREE

Training and Preparation

ONCE THE RECRUITS HAD SETTLED at Lower Fort Garry in November 1873, the officers could focus on molding them into Mounties. A "Daily Routine" was scheduled within a few weeks and, with minor revisions, would remain in place until late spring. Between 6:00 AM reveille and 10:00 PM lights out stretched hours of parade, equitation and guarding. Sub-Inspector John McIllree and Sergeant-Major A.H. Griesbach were in charge of discipline and foot drill, simple lessons for the many troopers with military experience. Major James Walsh and Sergeant-Major Sam Steele led equitation, and discovered that, despite claims made at the time of recruitment, few of the men had riding experience. In addition, Acting Commissioner Smith had aquired unbroken mustangs, which made equitation even more difficult. But Walsh and Steele, a hard-nosed veteran of the Red River Expedition, were equal to the task.

Little about Sam Steele wasn't larger than life. The man looked like a bull. Short, fine hair on his square head made for a generous face, fleshy like a sowbelly save for a small handlebar

The indefatigable Sam Steele (1849–1919) started his career in the NWMP as a sergeant-major and retired as a super-intendent in 1899.

moustache. His head sat atop a barrel chest without evidence or apparent need of a neck. Steele took on an undisciplined trooper, an opponent or a bottle of whiskey with the same sin-gle-mindedness and determination. Already the men marveled at his ability to put in long days, despite nights of carousing, in his determination to turn the men into riders.

"Our work was unceasing from 6:00 AM until after dark,"
described Steele in his journal. "I drilled five rides per day the
whole of the winter in an open menage, and the order was that
if the temperature was not lower than –36 °F the riding and
breaking should go on."

While the task tested Steele's resolution, it wasn't the hours
but the "performance" that he found most trying. As he
watched the troopers participate in the menage, a drill performed without stirrups and reins so as to improve balance
and skill, he wasn't sure if laughter or tears were appropriate.
He merely watched in disbelief, as only a few men remained
seated on their horse's backs. More common were those laid
out flat on the ground.

Occasionally a frustrated Steele would bellow a command.
"The order to dismount has not yet been given, sub-constable!"

He wasn't unsympathetic, however. To ease the pain of
landing on frozen ground, he covered it with fir branches to
break the men's falls. On occasion, he thought he'd made it
a little too comfortable.

"It's not meant to be a bed, constable," he barked at a trooper
who dallied too long on the greenery.

The humorous spectacle of troopers learning to ride proved
a popular draw for the men not training. They watched in
amusement as a greenhorn wrapped his arms tightly around
the horse's neck, usually with nose deep in the animal's coarse
mane. But Steele's hard work and discipline paid off, and
spring witnessed him declare, perhaps a little too enthusiastically, that the men were "very fine riders."

Most lessons took place in late winter and early spring after
the cold prairie winter released its harsh grip. By December, the
temperature regularly dropped below –36° F, which brought
parades, equitation and drills to a halt. The troopers would
have preferred a warmer cut-off, especially since the bulk of
their winter clothes remained packed in ice on the Dawson

Route. But as the environment grew more inhospitable, discipline was relaxed to allow the men some comfort, a trend most visible with the guards who were stationed around the fort. At first, they were allowed to place their hands in their pockets. Eventually, they could take shelter while on duty. Often they took advantage of the relaxation in rules; the stable guards covered themselves in hay and slept through the bitter nights, but only after ensuring that the lights in the Big House, the officers' quarters, were extinguished.

Given the Mounties' charge to enforce law and order in the North-West Territories, it might have been expected that they received some education in law or police procedures. Long winter hours spent indoors presented the ideal opportunity, but it didn't happen. Instead, the men faced days of drudgery, boredom and repetitive physical tasks.

Occasional skating parties with the Métis women from Red River broke the tedium. Acting Constable James Fullerton spoke for many of his fellow troopers when he declared that the events were much anticipated because a twirl with the local girls always made it feel warmer. Other young ladies were introduced to the officers through the Quadrille Club. But encounters were fleeting since the Mounties were not allowed to marry. Sam Steele set a singular example for the men by spending evenings among the Métis who lived in the vicinity, listening to stories about their culture and absorbing all he could about conditions in the West. Other officers could have benefited from following his lead.

Many troopers found relief from boredom and cold in vice. Gambling was common, but drinking was especially popular. Ironically, given the Mounties' charge to rid the West of whiskey traders, alcohol smuggling quickly emerged as a chronic problem. Leave from the fort was limited, so when granted rare hours of freedom, the men purchased enough alcohol to bring back to the barracks. By mid-December the officers ordered the practice prohibited. While it undermined the smuggling, the order didn't have much effect on drinking. The covert activity was quickly replaced by open-air purchases at the local HBC canteen, a popular establishment with off-duty troopers.

It was left to Commissioner George French, who replaced Acting Commissioner Osbourne Smith on December 16, to deal with these recurring problems. He appeared equal to the task. French was a model of refined contemporary tastes. Sideburns extended from a receding hairline, and a full handlebar moustache balanced between an ample nose and a strong chin. Officers and troopers would learn that in attitude and practice, French exemplified the aristocratic airs of Britain's military elite. He brooked no interference in how he ran his force, and he rarely questioned his own decisions or sought counsel from inferior officers. Those inclined to offer advice soon learned that the commissioner considered it both forward and meddlesome.

French formally addressed the men and the problem of drinking immediately after his arrival. "Many of you have been soldiers. I remind you that is no longer your role. You are members of the North-West Mounted Police. Habits that might have been tolerated among soldiers are not appropriate for police. Your task is to uphold the law. I hope that you will soon develop a guiding notion of self-respect, since it is hypocrisy to indulge in the practice for which you are to arrest others."

French expected his word to be received as law, and felt confident his direction would be followed.

Poor discipline was not the only problem to welcome Commissioner French to the Lower Fort Garry. He was greeted with a petition advocating the promotion of Sub-Inspector Brisebois to inspector signed by 30 members of the force. The petition had been forwarded to the Department of Justice prior to French's arrival, and the commissioner was incensed that the minister had seen fit to deal with the matter without his input.

French wrote a hurried and sharp letter to Hewitt Bernard noting his displeasure. French's rebuke resulted in the denial of Sub-Inspector Brisebois' promotion, and also set the stage for the acrimonious head-butting that was to characterize the commissioner's relationship with his political superiors for the duration of his command.

Upon his arrival, French also confronted rumors that whiskey traders were illegally trading liquor to Natives at Big Black Island on Lake Winnipeg. On December 11, the Council of the North-West Territories, the administrative body for the region directed by Lieutenant-Governor Morris, requested Smith to investigate. Smith did not believe that his organizational responsibilities included the authority to deploy the force, so he filed the request for French. When the Council made a second request, it admitted that details were sketchy, but apparently the whiskey traders used a lumber business as a cover and operated just outside the provincial boundary.

French thought the request fell within the force's mandate. He also saw it as an opportunity to demonstrate to the troopers the seriousness that must attend the force's dealings with alcohol. Because it would be the Mounties's first patrol, French realized that the matter of command was critical. When he considered the officers to lead the mission, his attention was drawn to Major James Macleod. At 37, the Scottish-born Macleod possessed a wealth of valuable experience. He had command experience, a higher education and a career as a lawyer. He seemed an ideal candidate.

Macleod accepted the command with enthusiasm. He had little trouble selecting nine men to form the patrol because the entire force was eager to participate. Training the volunteers to use snowshoes, which were necessary because the landscape was already blanketed in white, proved a greater challenge. Nestled warm in horse-drawn sleighs and with dogsleds pulling their supplies, the patrol left on December 29, fully expecting to arrest the culprits.

As the patrol approached Lake Winnipeg, Macleod called a halt and advanced onto the lake to test the ice.

"I don't want to take any chances on this ice, men," called Macleod, as he walked back to the shore. "It seems thick enough, but the weight of the horses may well crack it. Let's break out the snowshoes."

Snowshoes strapped to their feet, the men walked single file towards the island. In places, the frozen surface was swept clean, and the neophytes engaged in a most interesting snow-shoe ballet, performed to the tune of colorful metaphors and guffaws. Finally, they reached the island, where they saw a shack through the barren trees.

"Quiet, men," commanded Macleod. He surveyed the small camp as they approached. No footprints could be seen in the snow nor smoke drifting from the small chimney.

"Sergeant-major, come with me. Men, wait here," instructed Macleod. "Keep your eyes open for any movement."

The pair walked to the door. Macleod took off his gloves. He placed one hand on his revolver and banged on the door with the other.

"I'm Major James Macleod of the Mounted Police force. In the name of the Dominion government, I direct you to open the door and exit the building."

No answer. After a few moments silence, Macleod threw open the door and stepped into the cold, dark room. As the light filtered in through the entrance and Macleod's eyes adjusted, he scanned the room and found it empty. Bunk-beds were pushed against one wall along with a few makeshift chairs hacked from the trunks of large trees but little in the way of supplies. In one corner, a buffalo robe was thrown against the walls. Macleod found two five-gallon barrels underneath it.

He found an ax, split one open and was greeted with the unmistakable smell of whiskey.

"Here it is." He hoisted one up over his shoulder and directed the sergeant-major to take the open one outside.

"No one's inside, but whoever was here was trading liquor," Macleod informed the men. He later heard a rumor that an HBC employee had visited the shack a few days earlier and warned the traders of the arrival of the force. Perhaps the rumor was true. Despite company desires that the police force put an end to illegal whiskey trade, it was likely that some traders were quietly involved in the practice.

"Set fire to the shack," Macleod instructed one of the sub-constables.

As the fire engulfed the building, he directed the sergeant-major to spill the contents of the barrel on the ground. The men licked their dry, chapped lips longingly as they watched the cruel order carried out. Macleod began to empty the other barrel; but before all its contents were on the ground, he placed the barrel upright.

"Get out your cups, men. It's going to be a cold night, and we might as well take the edge off it."

"Hurrahs" sounded all around as Macleod filled each man's cup. The thoughtful act and subsequent discussion in the barracks back at the fort did much to elevate Macleod's standing among the men. Warmed by the fire and the spirits, they made their way back to their supplies and set up camp for the night. They returned to Lower Fort Garry on January 7, and Macleod's report to French likely did not include the whiskey they shared.

The commissioner, meanwhile, found his stubborn and bored troopers lacking in honorable conduct. His initial words had little effect on the men's drinking, so French adopted punitive measures. In mid-January 1874, he posted orders outlining fines for drunkenness. First offenders were fined $3, equivalent to a sub-constable's four-day pay, and for subsequent offenses, the fine was doubled. If a man showed up unfit for guard duty, the fine was a hefty $9. Drunk or disorderly troopers also faced confinement in the guardhouse, or for the most serious offenders, dismissal. Later in the month, French posted additional orders prohibiting gambling in the barracks. The commissioner especially wished to end gaming fraternization between the ranks, which he considered inappropriate.

Late winter brought warmer weather to Manitoba, and a more disciplined routine settled over the men in the Stone Fort. Drill and Equitation were cancelled less frequently, and the men's skills advanced accordingly. Long, warm days also increased the popularity of outdoor activities. The men held cricket matches, including a special contest between a team from the force and a local 11 to commemorate the Queen's birthday. Target competitions, enjoyable at first, faded in popularity as the men began shooting local game.

Others who tired of the routine, discipline and long weeks of harsh weather began writing home. In their letters, they often complained about the lack of supplies, the poor quality of food and the treatment they received—better fit for animals than men. French had used the inevitable challenging conditions to toughen up the men. Desertions occurred, as expected, but such departures weren't lamented. The last thing French wanted was malcontents on the march. As for those who had seen fit to complain but remain with the force, they would soon look back on those first months of training with fondness and longing.

After less than a month at Lower Fort Garry, Commissioner George French felt he had a sufficient handle on the force's training to return to Ontario, where he could address needs of additional recruits and supplies. French sought permission for the visit from Hewitt Bernard. The commissioner's frank letters to his political superior offered his view of the force, its mission and his own leadership style.

In late December French wrote,

> The officers are generally a good lot of fellows, the men are also, but 15 or 20 of them should never have been sent here, being altogether too weak. Thirty-eight horses have been purchased, but the animals are scarcely fit for our work. As far as I can see, we will require from 200 to 300 horses by next June, and all these must be brought from Canada or the States, as they are not to be had here. There will be hot work for us next summer. The governor [Morris] has had reliable information that there are five forts between the Milk River and Edmonton, one of them containing 100 outlaws and desperadoes, and mounting several guns. The manner in which they got the guns will give you some idea of the ruffians we will have to deal with; it was simply this: they assaulted an army train which the U.S. government was sending to one of their western forts, captured the guns and ran them across the line. They boldly give out that they will fight it out with any force that goes to disturb them, and as most of them had been outlawed in Montana, I think it is possible they mean what they say. I hope so. If the department lets me have two or three guns attached to my 300 men, I trust we will be able to make the rascals feel the strong arm of the law. You will see what an immense amount of work will have to be done by next summer, sending out such a force such a distance, and having to carry all our supplies with us.

French followed up with a second letter in mid-January, a full report on the requirements of the NWMP.

> I expect that if you agree with me in the necessity for immediate action, to receive a telegram from you, and to leave

here before the first of February. I would at once set to work
to raise some more men at Kingston or Toronto, and purchase
a few horses, leaving a good officer or two to carry on the drill,
etc. I would proceed to England about the first of March,
obtain all the necessary uniforms, saddlery, revolvers and
stores of various descriptions, and would return by the first of
May if possible....I regret to have to state that a large num-
ber of men sent here are quite unfit for the work. The doctor
thinks that about 20 will have to be rejected on medical
grounds, and I fear as many more will have to be dismissed for
misconduct. The fact is that the men were enlisted in too great
a hurry, and they fancy themselves to be more militiamen
than policeman. If, when in the Old Country, I had author-
ity to obtain 15 or 20 men from the Royal Irish Constabu-
lary, I could pick out the very best men, and they would make
a splendid leaven for the present unleavened mass.

French's letters arrived in Ottawa during a period of turmoil associated with the North-West Mounted Police, which for some weeks put the future of the force into question. The Pacific Scandal continued to dog Prime Minister Macdonald throughout the fall, and rather than endure the imminent defeat of his government in the House of Commons, his Cabinet resigned on November 5, 1873. The Liberals, led by Alexander Mackenzie, replaced the Conservative government, and A.A. Dorion was appointed Minister of Justice. While Mackenzie, a prohibitionist, was anxious to rid the North-West Territories of the whiskey traders, he did not believe that Macdonald's mounted police force could achieve it. Instead he proposed a joint Canadian-American expedition that authorized American troops to enter Canada and address the problem.

It was left to Governor General the Earl of Dufferin to explain to Mackenzie the flaws in his plan—the undermining of sovereignty over the North-West Territories and the possibility

Alexander Mackenzie (1822–92), Canada's second prime minister, questioned the need for the NWMP when his party formed the government in 1873.

~∽✕∾~

of Native warfare. Dufferin made his objections known to the new prime minister in a series of communications, in words that might easily have come from Macdonald save for the delicate tone required by the situation.

The governor general emphasized the importance of a Canadian force in the North-West Territories. In unassailable logic, he noted that if the Dominion lost the prairies to the United

States, British Columbia would be isolated and would soon follow. Without a hinterland to support eastern industry, Canada's economy would suffer. The Dominion would be forced into an undesirable continental arrangement with the U.S. Furthermore, allowing a foreign nation to control its own forces in Dominion territory would certainly not sit well with British authorities.

Dufferin was also wary of the impact blue-coated American soldiers would have on the local Native populations. There would be no enthusiastic reception. Natives undoubtedly knew the history of repression and violence of the United States military in the American West. He tactfully suggested that Canada's best objective was to restrain and control Native populations, not kill them. Certainly, Native willingness to sign treaties would not be enhanced with bloodshed. And if violence erupted, the Dominion government would inevitably find itself in a undesirable position, since without the funds to fight a Native war, American troops would likely address the problem in their own way.

Mackenzie listened to Dufferin's advice, and in January 1874 the prime minister decided that a wholly Canadian force could address the western problem, but he remained uncertain of the North-West Mounted Police's ability to handle the challenge. He preferred a joint military-police expedition, but military authorities were unenthusiastic about such an undertaking. The clincher in favor of the mounted police was the unwavering support it received in the Department of Justice, where the Deputy Minister, Hewitt Bernard, had survived the change in governments. Early in the new year Mackenzie capitulated; the North-West Mounted Police would march west.

Mackenzie, Dorion and Bernard agreed that French should come to Ontario to address the needs he'd identified, and he arrived in Ottawa on February 5. French had little difficulty convincing his superiors that it was necessary to increase the force to the maximum 300 allowed under the legislation. Reasonable men could see that the task was daunting enough. The Dominion government did not authorize his supply and recruitment trip to England because of time constraints. Dominion officials in England would secure supplies, but the infusion of Royal Irish Constabulary members would not be forthcoming.

French then turned to the important matter of procuring horses. He was an accomplished horseman, and few could question his judge of horseflesh. His comment to Bernard regarding the unsuitability of the mustangs already purchased was understated. French was aghast at the quality of the animals. Small and scruffy, they appeared suited for little more than pulling carts. He wanted horses from eastern Canada, imposing and graceful, such as his own chestnut thoroughbred Silver Blaze. He secured a few hundred thoroughbreds, all stable-raised and used to feed of grain and hay. The quality of the horses was not doubted, and knowledgeable horsemen thought they were the best animals to have been shipped out of Toronto at that time.

The horses' diet meant that they would need oats on the march west, and French was aware of the logistical problems posed by the transportation of the feed. At a minimum half ration of five pounds per day, he anticipated that the three-month supply would require over 400,000 pounds of oats and 81 Red River carts to move it. French did not consider the problem insurmountable, especially because he thought the animals could use the expected vast expanses of forage in the West to supplement the oats.

Others were less certain. Sam Steele, who was warned of the limitations of eastern horses by the local Métis, advised Commissioner French that it took at least a year for such animals to become acclimatized to eat forage. French ignored the advice. It was important that the force look professional, and the western mustang simply could not provide the desired appearance.

Meanwhile, recruitment of a second 150 troopers began. Inspector William Jarvis and Sub-Inspector James Walker had accompanied French to Ottawa, and they were responsible for the operation. In Toronto, news that the force was looking for recruits caught the attention of 15-year-old Fred Bagley, who wasted no time in enlisting. The teenager's father learned of his son's action from his old comrade Commissioner French. A heated discussion followed.

"You can't go. I won't allow it. It's that simple," the father declared.

"Father, I'm a man. I've a right to make my own decisions about my future. It's my life," countered the son.

"You're 15 years old and still wet behind the ears, boy!" exclaimed his father. "The journey will challenge the skills of even seasoned veterans. You're aware I speak with some authority on this. I've had to subdue more than my share of savages with Her Majesty's army."

"Please, Father. They're not savages, but noble beings untainted by our vices."

The father grunted. "Son, I know you're well versed in the works of that Cooper chap, but it's romantic fiction, utter nonsense. Damn it! I rue the day those books were brought into this house." He shook his head. "It's not romance you'll find on the frontier, but violence and desperation."

"Let me discover it for myself, Father."

Eventually, Fred's pleas eroded his father's will. The senior Bagley knew something about the sense of adventure that coursed through a young man's veins, and he had great respect for French.

"You've got a stubborn streak, boy. I'll not stand in your way. You can sign up as a trumpeter, but only for six months."

The boy embraced his father.

"Listen carefully, Fred," warned his father, with his hand placed upon the young man's shoulder. "I'm going to be frank, as men must be. The dangers on the frontier are not only found on the flint tip of the redskins' arrows. You've got to protect yourself against vices from within. There'll be squaws, and they'll be…available. If you succumb to temptation, you'll know pain you never dreamed possible. Understand, son?"

His father seemed to speak with some authority on this, and Fred nodded. Truthfully, he couldn't imagine such illicit affairs with pure, young Indian princesses; and to believe that they might be the source of such unfortunate consequences… well, that was simply impossible.

"I'll be careful, Father."

"Off with you then."

Fred set off for the New Fort in Toronto, where the second group of recruits would be trained, unaware he would not see his family for another 14 years.

When Fred arrived at the New Fort, he fell under the charge of Major James Walsh, whom French had summoned from Lower Fort Garry to assist with training. With characteristic vigor, Walsh quickly asserted himself, and the men came to realize that he was a force to be reckoned with. Despite Walsh's efforts, the training challenges common in Lower Fort Garry soon became apparent. Equitation instructors took pleasure in using heartless techniques to further the recruits' skill development. As the mounted men inevitably lost their balance, the instructors used whips to crack the flanks of the confused horses. The startled animals darted off to the stables, leaving bewildered riders with bruised tailbones looking skyward.

Commissioner French was, at the same time, preoccupied with other duties. The recruits marveled at his energy and presence. He directed all training efforts and disciplined the incompetent, advising those who were not up to the challenge to resign. French proved to be very much a "hands-on" commissioner, directly involved in all aspects of the force and reluctant to delegate responsibilities. In his view, the success or failure of the force personally reflected on him. French would have been the first to admit call himself a demanding authoritarian who refused to accept anything less than perfection. Others thought his demeanor cold and distant. His poor relationship with subordinate officers and the troopers drew hushed complaints that he cared more about his horse than he did the men.

Nevertheless, he did look out for the interests of those under his command. He secured appointments for additional officers and supported those with demonstrated ability. He recommended that James Macleod be appointed to the newly created position of assistant commissioner of the force, and James Walsh promoted to inspector. Both appointments were announced on June 1. He also recommended and secured pay raises for non-commissioned officers.

Still, notions of the necessity of hierarchy and appropriate military discipline were bred in French's bones, and they plagued his command. He also continued to butt heads with his government superiors. On May 28, he was informed that the Minister of Justice had selected the HBC post of Fort Ellice as the force headquarters. While Fort Ellice was well situated at the junction of the Assiniboine and Qu'Appelle Rivers along the Fort Garry–Fort Edmonton trail, French did not see the isolated northern post as a desirable headquarters. He wrote to Bernard:

> *The idea of wintering any large portion of the Force at Fort Ellice this winter is entirely out of the question. The Governor [Morris] entirely agrees with me as to the unsuitability of Fort Ellice as a headquarters for the Force. If the Department [of Justice] chooses to set his opinion and mine aside, they can do so, but they must take the responsibility thereof.*

I am making such arrangements I can, without expenses, to provide for the wintering of the Force at the Stone Fort, Winnipeg and Dufferin.

French's objections were noted but not acted upon. Fort Ellice would remain the headquarters of the mounted police force.

The second wave of recruits, Divisions D, E, and F—referred to as the left wing—prepared to depart Toronto on June 6, 1874. They would avoid the inefficient and grueling Dawson Route to Manitoba because the United States government had granted the force permission to travel by train to Fargo, North Dakota, via Chicago and St. Paul. Few Yankee onlookers, however, would have been able to identify the troops as Canada's mounted police force because American authorities demanded that they travel in civilian clothes with arms, ammunition and equipment packed in freight cars. Once in Fargo, the troops would march north to Fort Dufferin, a Hudson's Bay Company and Boundary Commission post just north of the international border, where Divisions A, B and C would meet them.

Commissioner George French was as enthusiastic as anyone on the day of departure, but the reserved bearing he considered appropriate for a commanding officer gave little indication of it. French decided that the sunny Toronto day provided an ideal opportunity for the left wing's first test as an entire unit. A commanding officer more familiar with his men might have thought differently. The previous evening, the men had celebrated in several grog shops around the New Fort. With the celebration's effects still lingering, the men were assembled on the parade grounds when French, high atop Silver Blaze, pranced onto the grounds. As usual, his horse was immaculately turned out, mane and tail braided and coat brushed to a high gloss. In his scarlet Norfolk jacket, blue trousers with a double white stripe, polished high black boots, white helmet and sword, French did his mount no shame.

French took his position near the front of the troops and called out his instructions. They were immediately followed by...nothing. Absolutely *nothing*. French's head jerked left and right as he scanned the parade grounds, but not one officer met his gaze. The recruits looked simply bewildered. French's face darkened to match the shade of his jacket. The commissioner barked his orders again. This time, the inspectors relayed the directions to the men, but in a scene reminiscent of the tower of Babylon, each officer evidently heard a different command, and the parade ground became a sea of chaos. French's jacket paled in comparison to his complexion, and his eyes bulged under the strain. Fortunately, quick-acting sergeants-major waded into the crowd, and with liberal use of brutal language and stinging cracks, forced the men into proper position. As they marched from the field, the officers sheepishly took up the rear, cursing the demon rum.

The contingent of 201 men, 16 officers, 244 horses and their equipment marched through Toronto to Union Station where a large crowd of family, friends and curious onlookers had gathered to see the force off.* A military band played lively tunes; final hugs, kisses and handshakes were exchanged. As the men boarded the two trains, they could hear cries of advice and goodbyes. When the trains pulled out of the station, the band broke into *Auld Lang Syne*, and rockets blazed into the air.

---

*Added to those at Lower Fort Garry, the recruits brought by Commissioner French exceeded 300 authorized by legislation. French anticipated that more would quit or desert and had brought an additional 20 men. He did not want the force to be undermanned.

Henri Julien's drawing of the NWMP loading horses bound for the West in boxcars at Toronto, June 1874. Commissioner French was disappointed when he saw the smallish and unimpressive western mustangs that were selected for use on the march, and he insisted that thoroughbreds from eastern Canada supplement the force's herd. The 278 horses acquired by French were top quality, but some voiced concerns about whether they would survive the march. French himself recorded a most ominous prediction offered by a man familiar with the western territory: "Well, if you have luck, you may get back by Christmas, with 40 percent of your horses." The march proved difficult on the animals, but in the opinion of John Poett, the force's veterinary surgeon, the cause was lack of good feed rather than French's choice of animals.

The journey through Chicago and St. Paul was uneventful, save for Fred Bagley's sighting of the outlaw Frank James, an encounter that stoked his already hot romantic notions of the mission. The troops reached Fargo on June 12, and all that remained was the march north to Fort Dufferin. As the men unloaded the equipment, they discovered that the wagons, disassembled for transport, had been stored haphazardly. Rather than placing all the parts for a complete wagon in one boxcar, the parts were scattered throughout the trains. The men were forced to lay all the pieces on the ground and construct the wagons as if building a puzzle. And while they had some notion of the finished product's appearance, few men had any idea how to reach that point. However, the dampened spirits of the troopers were raised when they discovered that the officers were equally ignorant.

The local residents looked at the equipment strewn across the countryside and let out a few guffaws. They bet on a long delay for the force at Fargo, and few troopers would have disagreed. But Commissioner French was undaunted. With great faith in proper organization, he set up a rotating four-hour schedule, and within a day, the wagons were assembled. The next evening the left wing moved out, proud of its efficient and seemingly well-seasoned efforts. Their steps were light, but they soon grew heavy as the troops encountered problems that would become all too familiar over the next months.

Sub-Inspector James Walker watched as a horse-pulled cart bolted off out of line.

"Rein the beasts in!" he called to the constable, who had clearly given up his attempt to control the horses in favor of simply staying on the cart. "Don't let them take the lead!"

Even as he gave the directions, Walker knew it was a lost cause. Only a day into the march, it was apparent the commissioner had erred in his selection of horses, although none would suggest it in his presence. While the animals were fine stock and well bred, the thoroughbreds were not trained to work in harness and would not pull the wagons. Walker ordered a team of men on horseback to chase down the wagon, an order much repeated over the following days.

French was aware of the limitations of the horses. He purposefully ensured that the weight of each cart was not burdensome, although others in the force thought even those loads excessive for the inexperienced animals. The strain on the animals was not helped by the hurried pace at which the commissioner drove the troops north. He was anxious to get back on Canadian soil and to begin the journey west. Often the daily march exceeded 35 miles. The veterinary surgeon of the force, John Poett, observed that the rigorous daily schedule was proving too onerous for the horses. The death of two animals and the disabling of countless others seemed to bear out his words. Poett worried that the animals might not recover for the march west. Others were concerned the animals might not be sufficiently acclimatized for the journey, when conditions would worsen.

Another demoralizing problem was food. Troops march on their stomachs, and while French was certainly aware of the dictum, he evidently failed to put it into practice. Only days into the march to Fort Dufferin, the men grumbled about their meals.

"I hope we'll not be living on wet and dry for the next three months," moaned Fred Bagley after he washed down the last of his piece of hardtack, a rock-like biscuit, with a swallow of tea. "It's not much of a meal."

"Now I know why the plates are so small," commented Edward Maunsell, a raw constable from Ireland. "It's to make the slice of fat bacon and the couple of biscuits look bigger." The chuckling that followed Maunsell's observation was silenced abruptly.

"By God," barked Sergeant-Major Bray. "Before long, you young pups'll remember these meals as some of the best you ever ate."

He was right. Although few recruits would have guessed it, the march west would see them pine for the meals eaten en route to Fort Dufferin.

When French and the left wing arrived at Fort Dufferin on June 19, the North-West Mounted Police force was finally assembled as a unit.* A, B, and C Troops had left Lower Fort Garry on June 7 and reached Fort Dufferin the previous day. The short southern journey along the Red River should not have taken 11 days, but the men shared the left wing's transportation problems. Carts broke down, and oxen ran off regularly. The camp, at least, looked welcoming thanks to Inspector Jacob Carvell and a dozen men who had been preparing the place since May.

It was impossible, however, to prepare for all contingencies, especially if Mother Nature intervened. On June 20 the force witnessed one of the most violent thunderstorms in local history. Lightning blanketed the sky like a bleached cotton sheet, and thunder boomed, reminding the force's war veterans of hotly contested battlefields. The horses French brought were corralled inside a ring of loaded wagons where they remained surprisingly calm for a few hours. Then, as Sam Steele describes, disaster struck.

---

* The force lacked Sub-Inspector Albert Shurtliff and 10 men, who had been dispatched to Fort Ellice in early May. Shurtliff was charged with checking carts along the Fort Edmonton–Fort Garry trail for illegal liquor and growing crops for the members of the force who were to return in November.

Henri Julien's drawing of the NWMP horse stampede during the June 1874 thunderstorm at Fort Dufferin

A thunderbolt fell in the midst of the horses. Terrified, they broke their fastenings and made for the side of the corral. The six men on guard were trampled underfoot as they tried to stop them. The maddened beasts overturned the huge wagons, dashed through a row of tents, scattered everything, and made for the gate of the large field in which we were encamped. In their mad efforts to pass they climbed over one another to the height of many feet....The stampede continued south across the Pembina bridge. Crazed with fright the horses crossed the river and continued their flight on the opposite bank, and the majority was between 30 and 50 miles in Dakota before they were compelled by sheer exhaustion to halt.

The next day Fred Bagley joined the others in the grueling task of tracking down the horses. Fortunately, the men could use the mustangs; they had been corralled away from the thoroughbreds and had not spooked during the storm. After 24 hours tracking the horses over a good 120 miles, which saw all but one of the animals recovered, Bagley was exhausted.

"Not much Fenimore Cooper romance about this," he scrawled in his diary.

There remained organizational work to complete before the North-West Mounted Police left Fort Dufferin. Troopers were transferred from the left wing to bring A, B and C Troops up to strength, about 50 men each. They loaded the supplies for the journey on the 73 wagons and 114 Red River carts. The artillery division under the command of Inspector William Winder, C Troop, considered the challenges of transporting the force's two nine-pound muzzle-loading guns. Each weighed 3800 pounds and needed to be pulled by four horses. Given the reports of the armed and fortified whiskey traders, French considered the artillery essential.

Commissioner French reviewed the details of the journey with Lieutenant-Governor Morris in Winnipeg. Morris had renewed concerns that Natives in the U.S. might ride north and incite Natives in the North-West Territories to war. He was also worried about the effect of the force's arrival on the Natives and that the Boundary Commission's work in the West, combined with the presence of an armed force, might arouse Native suspicion, inflame passions and result in violence. Morris and the Council of the North-West Territories recommended to the Dominion government that a trustworthy individual be dispatched to inform the Native populations of their intent.

French thought the idea a good one, as did the Dominion government. Reverend John McDougall was speedily dispatched. "Parson John" was born and raised in the West and had long experience as a missionary there. With his Bible at his side, he feared no man. His bravado and temperament had earned him the respect of Cree and Blackfoot alike, a rare accomplishment. He was charged with explaining to the Natives that the North-West Mounted Police was coming to preserve law and order and remove the plague of the whiskey traders. They were a mark of the Great White Mother's (Queen Victoria) good will and would promote Native happiness. McDougall was also given access to HBC's trade goods, to use at his discretion to make his case more convincing.

The commissioner and the lieutenant-governor also finalized the journey's itinerary. While in Ottawa in late winter, the Department of Justice directed French to march the force across the plains from Fort Dufferin to Fort Whoop-Up, which was believed to be at the junction of the Bow and Belly Rivers. Once the fort was closed down, half of the force would winter at Fort Edmonton, and the remainder would return to Fort Ellice. Fears of contact with hostile U.S. Natives active along the border, especially the Sioux, changed the anticipated route. The force would travel along the international boundary for 200 miles and then take a more northerly route towards the Qu'Appelle River. Before they reached the river, they would turn west towards the Cypress Hills. Despite the Department of Justice's directions, French remained determined to winter the part of the force that did not remain in the far North-West Territories at Winnipeg and Fort Dufferin.

French was anxious to get the force out of Fort Dufferin. Several low public houses served the community and proved too attractive to the men and some officers. Inspector Charles Young drank to excess with unfortunate results. French was forced to dismiss him for "using grossly insubordinate language to the Commissioner when on duty." The cooks also had difficulty mastering their art, which was the source of much grousing among the men. Complaints undermined the esprit de corps that had been forming.

"To get badly cooked food, to be worked hard all day and to be pestered all night by mosquitoes is objectionable," noted French, "and it is not encouraging to an ordinary individual, under such circumstances, to be assured by one of these prophets of evil who are always about (but who, unfortunately, do not always flee from the misfortunes they predict)."

Regrettably, unanticipated delays occurred. A large quantity of oats and flour had been damaged or lost on the Red River during transportation from Fargo. The Boundary Commission eventually replaced the flour, but the horses would have to do with limited oats for feed. The force also had to wait for the delivery of revolvers from the military in Britain. The enthusiasm that greeted the arrival of the crates in late June dissipated when they inspected the weapons. The 330 Adams revolvers were poorly packed and in worse shape. Ramrods were bent, screws had worked loose, and many revolvers were simply broken. The force armorer was able to cobble together a few workable revolvers, but most of the men went without side arms unless they had their own. The rifles, Snider-Enfield carbines cast off by the British Army, were not much better. They were converted to breech loaders, but only accurate up to about 200 yards.

Commissioner French gave orders that the force would be moving out on July 6. At a final parade on July 3, French took the opportunity to address the troops.

Men, I will speak plainly because you have a right to know what lies ahead. It is not a journey for boys, and many men might justly consider whether they are suited for it.

There will be plenty of hardship. You might be wet day after day and have to sleep in wet clothes. You may well go a day or two without food, and I fear that you will often be without water. We must pass through Blackfoot country, warlike Indians well known for their antipathy towards white men. And then there will surely be hot work when we find the whiskey traders.

Any members who are not prepared to take their chances of these privations should fall out. There is no disgrace, and there will be no penalty.

The men had heard this speech numerous times, and most were suspecting that it might be accurate. Some surely contemplated joining those who had quit, but none fell out on the parade grounds. But when the force began its march, 31 men had deserted, or taken "French leave" as the men called it. Undoubtedly, some based the last-minute decision on news of a recent Sioux raid on the nearby American settlement of St. Ive, near Fort Pembina. The Sioux action delayed the departure of the force by two days to July 8, as the commandant of Fort Pembina asked Commissioner French for its support should the Sioux continue their attack. They did not. As for the deserters, the commissioner thought it best they take their leave.

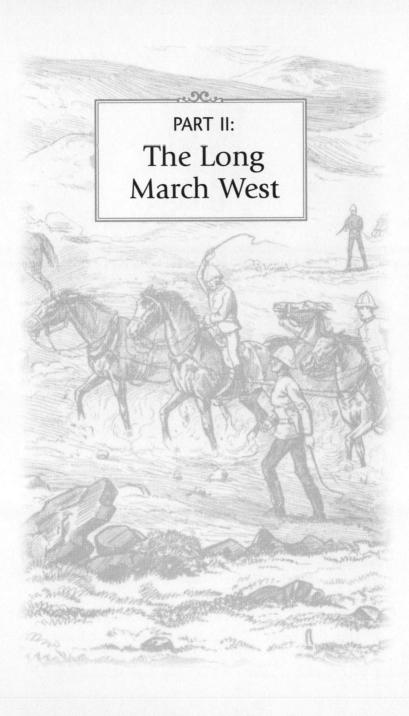

PART II:
The Long March West

CHAPTER FOUR

Fort Dufferin to the Souris River

Day 1, Fort Dufferin
2 Miles Traveled
ON JULY 8, THE NORTH-WEST MOUNTED POLICE made final preparations to march west. Fred Bagley, B Troop's young bugler, stifled a yawn from atop his fine chocolate brown horse at the head of the 50 or so men in his division. He'd been too excited about the force's departure to sleep the night before. But his excitement waned as the day slipped by. As he looked around at the two-mile long procession of men, animals and equipment that spilled out of the Commission Campground, he noticed that the shadows were growing long. He turned back and shifted in his British Army pattern saddle, which still hadn't shaped to anything near comfortable. At least he had good horse to ride. Bagley chuckled as his thoughts drifted to how he had acquired the animal.

He'd been shocked to discover the condition of the horse that he was initially assigned on his arrival in Fort Dufferin. That animal sagged when mounted and creaked at a trot. Bagley refused to push it to a full gallop because he feared it might drop dead under the increased strain. Clearly, the animal wouldn't do. It wasn't likely to last the march, and more importantly, no self-respecting Indian princess, even *if* in need, would be seen upon it. So Bagley spent his free time searching for a suitable mount. A few days before departure, he caught sight of a most magnificent animal that might have leapt from the pages of a Fenimore Cooper novel. He scouted the animal for a while and smiled when he saw its drunken owner lurch towards it. Bagley approached the Mountie and convinced him to borrow some money for another drink. When the happy man stumbled back inside a grog shop, Bagley mounted the horse and sped away, sure that the animal was his to keep. Everyone knew Commissioner French didn't tolerate drunks, and the victimized sub-constable wasn't likely to tell anyone that the horse disappeared while he was sober. Bagley felt somewhat guilty, but reassured himself that a western hero in similar circumstances would do the same.

"You look like the cat that's swallowed the canary, boy," observed Sergeant-Major Joseph Francis.

Bagley's smile disappeared, and the blood drained from his face. For a moment he thought that Francis, a Crimean War veteran, had read his thoughts.

"Not feeling poorly, are you?" asked a suddenly puzzled Francis.

"Just eager to get moving, sir," replied Bagley. "I can't figure out why we're leaving so late in the day. We're not likely to get far before sundown."

"That's the whole point, son. It's called a Hudson's Bay start. The idea is to travel a few miles, trying out the new equipment without putting too much stress on it. If we discover we're carrying too much, we can easily return the excess to Fort Dufferin. And we don't have to worry about leaving anything of importance behind because it'd be a short trip to retrieve it."

The young, romantic Fred Bagley (1859–1945) joined the NWMP at age 15 and enjoyed a 25-year career with the force.

"I get it. Just like the great fur-trading expeditions of the Hudson's Bay Company," said Bagley.

"Pretty much. Course, that only explains why they go just a few miles on the first day. The late start gives the Half-breeds plenty of time to sober up before they've got to do any work," chuckled Francis.

Bagley nodded. He didn't know much about the Métis. The force employed 20 cart drivers and a handful of guides, but they mostly kept to themselves. He'd occasionally ventured near their campfires at night, listening to their singing and story-telling. From what he could tell, they were an independent lot and didn't take orders well. Truth be told, Bagley was a bit wary of them.

"Look sharp, men," Francis barked to B Troop. "The commissioner's coming."

Commissioner George French was riding Silver Blaze along the column of men, a final informal inspection before giving the signal to march. He found it difficult to be overly critical of what he saw. There remained some inconsistencies in the uniforms, but the scarlet jackets, pale gray riding breeches, shiny black boots, tanned leather gloves and white pith helmets gave the force a splendidly official appearance that clearly set them apart from the blue-coated American military. The splendid array of muscular horses validated his decision to import the animals from Toronto. He was also pleased with his subsequent decision to sort the animals by color. The dark bays of A Troop led the dark browns of B Troop. The glossy chestnuts of the Artillery Troop C stood smartly near the middle of the column with the two big, burnished nine-pound guns. D Troop's grays and buckskins, the blacks of E Troop and the light bays of F Troop all followed behind.

It was unfortunate, French thought, that the ox-drawn Red River carts, piled high with supplies and manned by colorfully dressed, pipe-smoking Métis detracted from the force's

The Métis handled the Red River carts, as seen in this drawing by Henri Julien, much to the exasperation of Commisioner French.

appearance. And the column's authority clearly deteriorated near the rear, where the cattle and agricultural implements were located. But the cattle were required for food, and the ploughs and harrows would be necessary for growing crops when western posts were established. Despite the unsightly caboose, French felt confident that any witness observing the force and its weaponry would recognize the planning and organization that went into the enterprise and would conclude that the North-West Mounted Police was not to be trifled with. He had no doubt that they would do their duty to bring law and order to the North-West Territories.

When French reached the head of the column, he thrust his blade skyward. Quietly, he regretted the absence of an official photographer, which he sacrificed due to the prohibitive cost of transporting the necessary equipment. Surely, it would have been grand to record for posterity the moment and the man. French pushed aside the regrets as he brought down his sword and pointed it west. Assistant Commissioner James Macleod barked a command, and the bugles bellowed. The men were off. The march had begun!

The force's nobility at rest was swiftly forgotten. Some stubborn horses easily got the best of their tenderfoot riders, who desperately clung to the runaways. Any man unable to hold his animal found himself on the ground, spitting language not at all befitting a Mountie. Those wagons not controlled by Métis strayed from the column because drivers were unable to rein in the pigheaded oxen. Some teams kicked up clouds of choking dust while others tipped their carts, unceremoniously spilling loads. To add to the confusion, the commissioned and non-commissioned officers raced up and down the length of the column, shouting orders desperately trying to control the formation.

And then there was the noise! It assaulted the ears in a most uncivilized fashion, quickly rising over the din of officer, trooper and animal and overwhelming the combined force of their shouts, neighs and bellows. It was the music of the Red River cart, coming from the grinding of wooden axle against wooden wheel. Its shriek was unique to the prairies and singular in its torturous effect on the ear. And absolutely nothing could be done about it. According to the Métis, who used the cart as their main means of transportation, buffalo grease applied to the axle brought brief silence, but the mechanism soon became caked with dirt from the trail, inevitably causing it to break. For the duration of the journey, the men would be treated to the unwelcome concert of the carts.

Day 2, Marias River
5 Miles Traveled

Commissioner French's hopes for improvement on the second day of the march were dashed even before the men moved out. When French ordered Inspector Theodore Richer to choose quiet horses to pull equipment, the commander of F Troop suggested that such a use of saddle horses was unjustified. Richer instead provided raw, poorly broken horses to the detail. When two of the animals bolted and broke a mowing machine, French and Richer became embroiled in a loud and acrimonious argument before 100 men. The exchange ended only when French gave the order to arrest Richer for gross insubordination. When Richer retorted that he planned to inform his own highly placed friends in the government of what he considered the commissioner's deficient and lamentable command of the force, French had him unceremoniously escorted back to Fort Dufferin.

The situation didn't improve when a relative of Richer's, also a member of F Troop, decided that the treatment of the inspector was sufficient cause for him to change his own plans. The trooper was driving a wagon along the Boundary Commission Road, which skirted the line dividing Canada and the United States. He abandoned his wagon and made a dash for the United States. When news of the desertion made its way up the line to French, the commissioner rode back to speak to the man. Safe in territory that recognized neither the Queen nor the Mounted Police, the man told French to "Go to hell." The commissioner turned his horse and returned to the troops without giving the deserter a second look.

The Hudson's Bay start, at least, proved useful. Some unnecessary items, including two carts of syrup, were returned to Fort

Dufferin, and additional oats were collected for the westward-bound cargo. The troops spent the better part of the day redistributing supplies to ensure more even loads, and it was late afternoon before the force began moving again. Before long, the sun dropped to the horizon, and although French wanted to give the order to set up camp, the barren landscape forced him to hold his tongue.

A confrontation with one of the force's guides, a man known only as Taylor, soon loosened the commissioner's tongue. French berated him for leading the force to such a wasteland, devoid of fuel and water. Taylor gave a feeble excuse, but French was concerned. He had suspicions about the guides' abilities. They seemed too fond of drink and too ready to dance around his questions about the territory that lay ahead. French hoped their present predicament was not caused by the man's ignorance, but he was not confident. He barked an order to Assistant Commissioner Macleod. The force would backtrack a few miles to a more favorable campsite at a bend in the Marias River. As the men retraced their steps, they noticed sights that some worried might foreshadow events to come. A dead horse and three canvas-covered wagons, broken beyond repair, were abandoned near the trail. The day's march ended in the same miserable fashion in which it had started.

As the men made camp for the night, French issued orders to post a guard. He wanted 30 mounted men, working on a rotating schedule, to provide the sentry. It was an elaborate guard, but French considered it necessary because of the desertions earlier in the day. With Fort Dufferin so close, more men might be tempted to take their leave and not be as circumspect as Richer's young relative, taking needed equipment or horses with them.

Edward Maunsell was a member of the guard placed on first relief. He received clear instructions from his superior, Sergeant Belcher.

"Maunsell, ride out a few hundred yards. Patrol east to west and occasionally shout 'Number five, and all's well.' Got it?"

"Yes, sir."

"I hope so. It's pretty damn simple. You'll get your supper when you're relieved."

Maunsell rode out, and as dusk settled on the land, he heard the faint call, "Number four, and all's well."

It was the last thing he remembered until his horse tripped on the reins that had slipped from his hands. He shook himself awake. Finally alert, he could hear no reassuring call of any guard. The cloudy night was dark, and without bearings on the horizon, he had no idea where the camp was! He stayed stationary for the rest of the night, and at sunrise began to search for his fellow troopers. After a few hours, he stumbled upon Sergeant Belcher and some of the guard driving the cattle after the already-departed force.

"Maunsell," barked Belcher. "I've reported you as a deserter. Said that you took the horse, saddle, gear, everything."

"Me, desert? No, sir! I got lost in the dark, sir!"

Belcher sighed and shook his head. "Green as St. Paddy's shamrock," he muttered to himself. "Get to work driving the cattle, boy."

It was the last Maunsell heard of the incident. Relieved, he figured Belcher didn't have him arrested because he'd missed supper and breakfast.

Given the food, thought Maunsell, *I didn't miss much.*

Day 4, Grant's Place
18 Miles Traveled

A stranger arrived in camp, although few took notice of another Métis. But Sam Steele noted the man's presence. He had remained in contact with the informative Métis. One of the cart drivers suggested that the newcomer had troubling information. He had come from the Métis community of St. Joe, about five miles south. The Sioux had raided it the night before and killed several people. The Métis thought the Natives might be moving north.

Steele knew the information was significant enough for French's ear, but respecting the chain of command, he first took the details to William Jarvis, his immediate superior, inspector of Steele's A Troop. Jarvis directed him to report to the commissioner. French ordered distribution of extra rounds of ammunition, dispatched an advance guard for the march and doubled the nightly sentry.

Rumors of the Sioux presence and a possible battle enlivened the day's march, but no one saw any. By evening, the force reached the Métis settlement of Grant's Place, named after Charles Grant, the local tavern proprietor. The Métis employed by the force knew that Grant's grog shop was the last watering hole before the Cypress Hills, nearly 600 miles away. Grant smelled money, and he made sure the troopers knew it as well. Sensing trouble, French ordered the tavern off limits.

The Métis could not comprehend such a bizarre order. They took one look at the dusty horizon and headed straight to Grant's establishment. French shook his head, resigned to the Métis' lack of self-discipline and certain that they would never respect his orders. He hoped he would succeed in controlling his own men, and he directed Macleod to keep a close eye on them and place deserving names on report. But experience had also taught the commissioner of his men's fondness for booze; the threat of being placed on report might not deter those most determined to drink. So French approached Grant and asked him to refrain from selling booze to his men. Grant responded with disbelief. The Métis entrepreneur would sell to anyone willing to buy, and that proved to be most of the men. Troopers hatched schemes and struck deals, and despite the commissioner's order, most washed away the dust of the trail.

Perhaps it was the lingering effect of the booze or three days of biscuits hard enough to challenge both tooth and jaw, but later in the evening the men participated in a slaughter at odds with the civilized nature of their mission. They stumbled upon a slough full of ducks. Abandoning self-restraint, the men bounded into the shallow pit, found what they could to use as clubs and proceeded to slaughter the birds. Screams of triumph merged with thudding blows, cracking whips and terrified squawking. The slough quickly turned a muddy brown, tinged with the color of blood, all beneath a cloud of white, green and brown feathers.

James Macleod watched the onslaught from a nearby bank. He listened as some more refined members of the force called to those in the slough to move so they'd have clearer shots at the ducks. He was ready to halt the entire affair when he spotted young Fred Bagley, and he took a moment to chuckle at the men's unbridled enthusiasm.

"It's hardly funny, Macleod," came the stern voice of French, who had approached him from behind.

Macleod turned to his commander. "Sir?"

"It's bloody barbaric. The men are behaving like animals." The look on French's face revealed his displeasure and distaste. "I expect discipline from them."

"Sir, I agree. The display is hardly a civil one. But in the men's defense, sir, the first few days of the march have been hard on them. I thought it might do them good to blow off some steam and get fresh meat in their bellies."

"It's a damn poor sight, Macleod. I'll remind you that discipline is not only expected, but that the success of our mission demands it. I trust that you'll deal with this in the appropriate manner." French wheeled on his heels and walked away.

"Yes, sir."

It wasn't Macleod's first run-in with the commissioner since the beginning of the march. The assistant commissioner had suggested that the order of the march be altered, with the kitchen and tent teams riding before the active force so that prepared food and lodging awaited the men at the end of the day. French had testily insisted there be no changes in the order of the march, and Macleod felt that the commissioner had taken the suggestion as a personal slight. Unwilling to further anger his superior, Macleod made his way towards the men. He placed a few on report but later made sure that no man went without his fill of duck.

Day 5, Pembina Mountain Depot
9 Miles Traveled

Henri Julien, the young, enthusiastic illustrator from the *Canadian Illustrated News*, hired in lieu of an official photographer, had eaten duck before, and while he did not agree with the manner in which the ducks met their deaths, he had to admit that duck had never tasted so good. He also thought he was familiar with mosquitoes, but his experiences failed to prepare him for the type he encountered on the march. The insects were a regular topic of conversation among the men, and even with their broad and varied histories, not one could say they had ever encountered mosquitoes quite like those on the prairies. They were unequalled in ferocity, singular in tenacity and unrelenting in their attack.

The force had marched only a few days, but Julien had already come to know and cringe at the signs of the mosquitoes' dreaded arrival. As the sun dipped below the horizon, great dark clouds rose from the ground, thickening as they approached, an eerie, shimmering veil between land and sky. Their faint drone became a roar that drowned out all other prairie sounds. Then the attack began.

The mosquitoes had an uncanny ability to find flesh, and unsecured clothing provided doorways for torture. Julien soon discovered that waving his arms at the insects was not a good

Commissioner French wanted a photographer to accompany the NWMP on its march west, but realized that transporting the fragile, bulky equipment was impossible. To ensure a visual record of the enterprise French wrote to the manager of the *Canadian Illustrated News* inviting an artist employed by the magazine to participate in the march. The Dominion government provided the illustrator with a horse and a full outfit, and he was treated as a member of the staff, which meant a personal servant, private tent and special rations. The manager immediately thought of Henri Julien (1852–1908). Trained as an engraver and lithographer, he was skilled, young and single. Most importantly, he was anxious for adventure, as the manager determined after a graphic conversation with Julien where he outlined the possible dangers of the march.

idea because it was essential to keep the hands secure against the ears to prevent invasion. Even a primal scream brought no relief, since the mosquitoes saw a gaping mouth as a welcome site for further assault.

The mosquitoes also victimized the animals. Julien witnessed tormented horses and dogs howling in pain. Even the oxen's thick skin provided little protection against the more determined insects. Beasts that quietly suffered the expert cutting slashes of a Métis driver's leather bullwhip, slashes that easily raised welts the size of a man's wrist, bellowed in agony at the unrelenting attack of the mosquitoes.

"I guess what the Métis said back in Dufferin was right," muttered Julien's riding companion. "The mosquitoes back there were nothing compared to those out here."

"*Oui*," agreed Julien. "You know, I like to do a bit of fishing, and I have spent much time in the backwoods of Ontario and Québec, where the trees are thick and the bugs even thicker. Fighting off the mosquitoes was only a stalemate at best. *Oui*, I'd say they robbed me of at least half the pleasure of my trips; they were that bad. I never dreamed I would encounter any worse."

"You shouldn't have searched your dreams, Henri, but your nightmares."

"I guess so," chuckled Julien. "But at least there we had a fighting chance. Smoke from a fire kept many of them at bay. We piled those green boughs high, and our eyes watered like a crying baby's. But it was better than being eaten alive. Out here, it is hard enough to find wood to start a fire. You can forget about making smoke.

"A smoky fire would be pointless out here anyway," reflected Julien after a moment's silence. "There are so many insects that even a forest fire wouldn't stop all of them."

"And it's not just their numbers," added his companion. "They're bloody huge."

Henri Julien's drawing of the NWMP at the foot of the Pembina Mountains, Summer 1874

"You hitch a few of those up to the Red River carts, and we'll have no trouble moving our equipment."

The pair laughed but soon fell silent, each aware that their good humor would disappear as soon as they made camp and the bloodsuckers found their prey stationary.

The men could not predict that the ravenous creatures would emerge as only one of several strange insects on the prairies. This day the force camped near the Pembina Mountain Depot, set up by the Boundary Commission. The men were enjoying an uncommon rest, marveling at the seemingly end-less stretch of the blue sky, when clouds suddenly blew in from the southwest and let forth a deluge of hail. Those not on duty scampered and plunged into their tents for protection, none too certain that the shelters could withstand the onslaught.

Sam Steele took to the protection of canvas. Although the hail fell heavily, he could see from the light on the tent that the clouds were breaking. Strangely, the rhythm of falling hail remained. Steele popped his head out through the tent's opening.

"Grasshoppers!" he shouted.

They were everywhere. Billowing clouds of insects drew his eyes skyward, and he marveled at the prismatic colors of the sun's rays glistening off their vibrating wings. With some effort, Steele pulled his eyes back to the camp. The grasshoppers seemed to particularly enjoy the paint and woodwork of the wagons, making the equipment appear to come alive. Sud-denly, the seriousness of the situation became clear.

"The tents," he shouted, and bolted from his own shelter. "We've got to pack the tents. The grasshoppers will destroy them!" A second troubling thought arose. The insects had come from the west. Would there be any fodder left for the animals to eat farther along the route?

Steele ran through camp to circulate his order, each step marked by the sickening crunch of squashed bugs. As the camp became more animated, a slippery layer of dead grasshoppers quickly covered the ground. The men might well have been back on the frozen Red River.

The speed with which the men disassembled and packed the tents showed improvement in that task. Increasingly, they worked in teams, efficient in purpose and practice. With all the work done, the men settled down to supper, which was plain water the color of tea and dry, hard biscuits.

"Let's just hope we don't see the rest of the plagues that visited Egypt," muttered one of the constables.

"Well, we sure as hell know what the famine's like," replied another and half-heartedly threw the shattered pieces of his rationed biscuit at the grasshoppers.

Day 6, Calf Mountain
17 Miles Traveled

George French was frustrated with the Métis' work ethic. Rarely did their supply-laden Red River carts begin marching with the troops. As a result, they arrived late to camp, and the men often went hungry well into the night. And the Métis seemed not to care for their animals, casually and regularly driving them through the hottest part of the day. But their insolence was most frustrating. If they didn't like an order, they waited until the commissioner's back was turned and then muttered away in their irritating patois. The more brash among them didn't even wait until he turned away. The Métis got away with their lax practices and trying attitudes because they had the upper hand. French couldn't do without them, and he had no authority to impose any code of discipline on them. But he had other options, and he gave orders assigning sub-constables as additional Red River cart drivers.

French realized that the men lacked experienced, but knew they would obey orders. They might also set an example for the Métis. Few men, however, were pleased with the new assignments. Although none said it to the commissioner's face, more than one commented that he had signed up as a member of a *mounted* police force and expected to ride horses not carts. They certainly opposed being placed on the same footing as the Métis, who had signed on with the force out of mere pecuniary interest. Furthermore, the Métis earned three times and more than the sub-constables! French was aware of the complaints even before Macleod brought them to his attention.

He did not appreciate the unsolicited input of his assistant commissioner.

Still, French admitted that the transition from horse rider to cart driver was not easy for many men, and he also recognized that the seemingly uncomplicated task was a challenge.

"It's easy enough, Sub-Constable Bagley," explained the staff sergeant. "If you want the oxen to go right, shout 'Gee,'" and if you want them to go left, shout 'Haw.' Take this stick and give them a good poke to get them moving."

Bagley took the stick and tapped his finger on the tip of the small spike at its end. "This won't hurt 'em?"

"It'll be like a love tap on their thick hides, boy."

Bagley had been reassured that the oxen were docile animals, but as a city boy, he continued to fear the big beasts. His confidence grew as he sat on the Red River cart behind the two oxen. They lumbered along, seeming disinterested.

This isn't so bad, thought Bagley. *Sure beats pulling a detail cutting hay for the horses.*

Then he got cocky.

"I believe I'll speed this up a little," he mumbled to himself and took his stick and gave the lead ox a jab in the rear flank. The animals took off at a speed he had not believed possible for the stubby-legged, barrel-like creatures.

"Holy hell!" shouted Bagley, as he tried to reposition his bouncing bottom on the seat. "Gee! Haw!"

The commands were ineffective and quickly replaced with words that would make his mother blush. A quick glance over his shoulder revealed most of the cart's load spilled out on the ground. Once he regained some stability, he struggled to rein in the beasts. He quickly discovered the futility of his efforts and resigned himself to settle in for the ride.

"If I can't stop you, I guess the Rocky Mountains will!"

Bagley didn't have to wait quite that long.

"Out for a little joy-ride, Sub-Constable Bagley?"

Major Macleod rode up from behind, grabbed the reins and brought the animals to a sudden halt.

"Sir, I—," muttered Bagley.

"No need to explain, boy," came the quick response. "Let's get back to the main body, and I'll send some men out with you to retrieve the scattered supplies."

Edward Maunsell had no ambition to be anything more than the sub-constable he was. He had long ago decided to take the line of least resistance—do what you're told and keep your head low so you won't be told to do too much. He didn't raise a peep when he was assigned cart-driver duty and was happy to discover that the work wasn't too demanding. He managed to drive the oxen without the problems he'd seen others endure. When he arrived in camp, he turned his ox loose to graze with the others then settled in for a nap before dinner. The voice of Sub-Inspector John French, the brother of the commissioner, woke him.

"Cripes, man, your ox has eaten its harness!"

Maunsell looked at the animal. Sure enough, its collar was a third of the way down its bulging throat. He jumped up and engaged in a tug of war with the beast. For some time the outcome was uncertain, but finally, the ox let go. Maunsell looked at the mangled collar, dripping with saliva. The stuffing was gone, and the end that had been in the ox's mouth was so thoroughly chewed that the equipment could no longer be used.

"What am I going to do, Jack?" he asked the sub-inspector, who was a friend and much less intimidating than Commissioner French.

"Why don't you take it to the Half-breed camp and try to *borrow* a replacement?"

Maunsell nodded. "Good thinking."

He found the Métis drivers asleep under their carts. They looked so peaceful that Maunsell didn't want to waken any of them, so he merely exchanged his damaged collar for another.

Day 7, Pembina River
16 Miles Traveled

On Tuesday, July 14, George French stood on the west bank of the Pembina River, just above what was known locally as the Pembina Crossing. It seemed a poor location to ford the river, but as the commissioner scanned the valley, he saw no more favorable place. His immediate problem was getting the horse-drawn wagons across. The bank where he stood dropped sharply to the water, and the horses made more progress slipping backwards than they did edging forward. The ridge on the far side looked almost as precipitous, and the horses faced similar problems navigating its slope. The march would be delayed until the oxen from the rear could replace the horses.

The day wasn't without good news, though. Pierre Lévéillé arrived with five men and five carts loaded with trade goods and gifts for the Natives. More importantly, Lévéillé was the force's chief guide and interpreter. French was pleased to see him, having lost confidence in the other guides. The Métis guide came highly recommended by Lieutenant-Governor Morris. Apparently, Lévéillé was a prairie hero whose father had served under Napoleon in the French army and whose mother was a mixed-blood daughter of the explorer Alexander Mackenzie. The others had equally impressive backgrounds. Genthon served as a guide for Sanford Flemming on his Pacific Railway expedition. Morin was an old-timer reported to have hunted buffalo since the dawn of the century. The Scottish Métis Welsh was supposedly born in the previous century and could speak a handful of Native languages.

French was concerned, however, about a troubling rumor that Morris recommended Lévéillé because he was one of the few Métis to oppose Riel during the Red River Rebellion. And that the man was Métis caused further concern. How was it possible that these people of the Plains could have survived and flourished for the better part of a century with the attitudes they demonstrated? Lévéillé would have the opportunity to prove himself, but French wished that the mission did not depend upon him.

Day 12, The Souris River
Rest Day

"Boy, oh boy!" shouted Fred Bagley as he splashed buck-naked in the clear Souris River, enjoying the Sunday without travel. "Where are the angels 'cause I gotta be in heaven!"

It was July 19, and Bagley relished the relief of the fast-flowing cool current on his skin. He might have scratched the insect bites that covered his body for days and it wouldn't have felt as good. He scrubbed the thick layer of prairie dust off, marveling at the hint of pink still beneath. But truth be told, he was most grateful for the opportunity to clean his soiled pants. The days that followed his feast of duck and muddy tea brought discomfort he'd never experienced. Embarrassed, he spoke of the problem to the good Major Macleod.

"Boy, the arsehole isn't here that's not screwed tighter than my old Scottish grandfather, God rest his soul. But there's few with his constitution, and you can be sure that you're not the only one who'll lose that battle," he said. Bagley was consoled more by the mud the major smeared as camouflage on the rear of his pants than by the Major's words.

Dr. John Kittson, the force's surgeon, had been working on a remedy to the problem, which, as Macleod suggested, had affected most men. He had expected there might be some stomach problems after the sudden consumption of fresh meat. Already, the stomach ailments had turned into an epidemic of diarrhea, or prairie cholera as the doctor called it. Kittson knew it would only intensify, especially because his efforts to find a cure had been unsuccessful. Both opium and

Ipecac proved useless. Finally, he settled on Trinitrate of Bismuth. He tripled the normal dosage, supplemented it with a pinch of opium and waited for the results. He felt confident that the men wouldn't be overly concerned that their stool was black as long as it was solid again.

But only the sickest worried about such things on this day because rest and relaxation were the orders from above. After Divine Service in the morning, which the devout commissioner insisted upon each Sunday, he had declared that the men would be allowed a full day of rest. The break also allowed the blacksmiths and wheelwrights to repair the equipment. John McIllree, sub-inspector of E Troop, thought the decision was a timely one. That morning, the men of E Troop had refused to march. They had turned in the previous night with empty stomachs because the supply carts were miles away. Sharp rocks peppered the ground, making sleep difficult. In the predawn hour, they were tired, hungry and cranky. When informed that the sleeping cooks had only arrived a few hours earlier and that they'd ride on a bellyful of cold tea, the men of E Troop decided they wouldn't ride at all. The situation had the potential for a rebellion. Inspector Jacob Carvell, E Troop's commander, defused the situation by scrounging up some rations.

McIllree tried to forget the unpleasant episode by signing out some fishing tackle to try his luck. He wet his line for a few hours and was rewarded with not so much as a bite. But poor fishing was forgotten as he made his way back to camp. He was welcomed by a smell that made him salivate like a mad dog— beef sizzling on the fire! Unmistakable! His leisurely gait turned into a jog.

Some men had questioned Commissioner French's decision to include a herd of cattle on the march to provide food at the western posts and occasionally during the march. And as his critics anticipated, the herd couldn't keep up with the marching force, and the meat on their ribs melted away with the rapid pace. French detailed men to guide the herd and keep it moving, a strategy that brought its own problems. Inevitably, they arrived in camp long after the nightly meal was eaten. Occasionally, the stragglers were desperate enough to scavenge supposedly secured stores. Given French's harsh regimen of punishment, this practice was not without its risks and more often than not, the men chose to go hungry.

But there were no complaints on this day, as the men feasted on red meat and washed it down with their fill of fresh river water. Satisfied, they followed the meal with song and dance. A fife appeared, and tent pegs on a makeshift drum kept the beat. Those who still had tobacco smoked it. For the first time since the men had left Fort Dufferin, they went to their bedrolls content.

CHAPTER FIVE

From the Souris River to Old Wives Lakes

Day 15, The Souris River
22 Miles Traveled

As THE FORCE REACHED the western bend of the Souris River on Wednesday, July 22, French breathed a sigh of relief when he saw that the banks weren't steep. Still, fording the 10 yards of strong current would be a challenge. More than one trooper fell, and French thanked a Métis driver who leaped from his cart to save a drowning sub-constable.

Greater problems appeared as the Souris River faded into the distance. Even with the two days rest, many horses were too exhausted to proceed. When the force broke camp, they left two horses behind, and two others had died. In the oppressive heat of the day, 15 animals failed to reach camp with the force. Exhaustion and heat were compounded by hunger because the ground was dry, grasshopper ravaged and mostly dirt. But grass would have been of limited value, and even French admitted that the eastern horses did not take well to it. They had nearly exhausted their supply of oats, and even though French knew it would be possible to purchase some from the Boundary Commission along the way that didn't help him solve the immediate problem. Most ominously, bleached buffalo bones were a common sight; their eerie white presence gave testament to nature's power. Unspoken fears that the bones of the force's own animals would soon dot the landscape of the prairie troubled French and the men and sparked a sense of urgency.

The situation required drastic action. French called Macleod and gave the order. "Inform the men that they must dismount and walk every alternate hour to conserve the horses' energy. Ensure there is only one man on a wagon at any one time."

Macleod could see the solid reasoning behind Commissioner French's command. He had already tried to address the problem of the horses' fatigue. Initially, a single trooper, usually a sub-constable, manned the carts. Macleod had issued an order that placed a Red River cart under the responsibility of a six-man team. One trooper would drive, while the other five sat in the back with the riderless horses were strung out behind the cart. French had criticized the arrangement because it failed to portray the visual standard he believed necessary for the force. Macleod was forced to abandon the strategy and took it upon himself to ride with the rear of the column, where he could try to ensure that the supplies reached camp in a more timely fashion.

Macleod suspected French's approach would be looked upon much less favorably than his own, but he did as directed. He would not be one of those reprimanded or dismissed from the force under French's uncompromising hand, and he was willing to harbor grievances and obey questionable commands to ensure the future he had carefully planned with his fiancée.

But as French discovered, others were not as dutiful as Macleod. The commissioner rode back along the column, as was his practice, when he spotted a man hitching a ride on one of the cook wagons.

"Sergeant Smith, isn't it?"

"Yes, sir."

"You'll extricate yourself from that wagon or be placed under arrest."

"Sir, I joined a mounted force, not a foot one, and I'll be damned if I'll walk. Besides, I'm sick, and I won't get far."

French bristled at the disobedience but bit his tongue since he knew there was likely truth in the sergeant's words. Many men still suffered from the prairie cholera, so the commissioner gave him the benefit of the doubt.

"At least get out of sight in the front of the cart, man," he directed. "And keep your ride to yourself."

After the men set up camp that night, they were as tired as they'd ever been on the march. Swollen, blistered feet proved that riding boots weren't designed for marching. Lips and throats were red and raw. Sleep allowed the most ready escape. The situation was so bad that few complained about the food or lack thereof.

Even sleep would not come easily. Late in the day, the force came upon a camp of Boundary Commission workers cutting hay south of the border. They brought disquieting news.

"Sioux've been up this way."

"Recently?" asked James Macleod, the force's liaison and negotiator with the Boundary Commission.

"Not mor'na couple days ago. Threatened to lay waste to us boys, less we gave 'em some our supplies. That's why we ain't got much to sell ya."

Sub-Constable Pierre Lucas had reported seeing Sioux while on guard duty a few nights before. No one had believed him then. This night, French posted a double guard, and the men cuddled their rifles.

Day 16, Rivière des Lacs
15 Miles Traveled

Fred Bagley heard the rumors about the Sioux sighting and spent the day's march scanning the horizon, but by the time the force made camp that afternoon, all he had for his efforts were tired, strained eyes. Disappointed, he wandered through the camp and found himself back with the Métis drivers. Bagley's opinion of the Métis had changed since he was detailed to drive carts with them. They weren't nearly as intimidating as he'd believed. Indeed, they were a fun-loving people, always with good stories to tell. Once there, he discovered several troopers gathered around one Métis. Bagley shouldered his way into the group.

"The Cree, he finished by digging footsteps up and down the side of the hill. That is the story of Butte Marguee," concluded the Métis.

"Ah, Pierre, surely you don't expect us to believe that," said one of the listeners.

"You don't have to believe my words. Butte Marguee is just over there," he said, pointing to a hill in the near distance. "Come, I show you."

Bagley thought the proposal sounded exciting and tagged along. He was dying to know the details of the story he'd missed and asked a fellow sub-constable to fill him in.

"Pierre said that in the old days wars raged between the red men on the prairies. Two of the worst of enemies were the Plains Cree and the Mandan from Missouri. One day, a Cree spotted a Mandan perched atop this here hill, watching for enemies. The Cree snuck up on him, and brought the Mandan down with a single blow of a stone across the back of his skull.

"The Cree used his tomahawk to scratch the outline of the dead man in the hard clay." continued the Mountie. "Only he dug it about twice the size of his victim. He added giant footprints up and down the hill for good measure."

"Wow!" gasped a wide-eyed Bagley. "And that's what he's going to show us now?"

"Claims so."

Within a few moments, the group reached the location. Sure enough, the outline of the murdered Mandan was visible. Scattered rocks filled the depression made so many years ago—rocks covered in the rusty brown of dried blood.

"Look at those rocks!" Bagley exclaimed. "How'd they all get so bloody?"

"It's not blood, boy," laughed one of the troopers. "It's lichen."

"I think not," said the Métis. "Surely, 'tis the blood of the dead man."

One of the men reached down and retrieved a stone the size of a fist near the head of the outline.

"Many men have passed this way," said Pierre. "Few have had the courage to disturb what is here. Bad medicine, 'tis said." With that, he turned and walked away.

The trooper who picked up the rock took a closer look at the object and let it fall gently to the ground. For a split second, Bagely thought about picking it up. But he knew something of the mystery of the Native peoples and decided that it was best to leave it. He was still wondering if it was the right decision when the force made camp that evening at Rivière des Lacs.

Day 17, Short Creek, near La Roche Percée
26.5 Miles Traveled

It wasn't even 3:00 AM, but Sergeant Major J.B. Mitchell of E Troop was awake and preparing for the day's march because he had some particularly motivating intelligence. Mitchell had learned from the example of Sam Steele and become good friends with the Métis guides, especially Lévéillé. He listened carefully as the guides discussed the condition of the next day's trail. If Mitchell discovered that the trail was well beaten, he took advantage of it and had E Troop ride at or near the front. If new ground had to be broken, Mitchell held them back and let the other troops do the hard work. Rarely was Lévéillé wrong, and Mitchell felt the information was valuable.

Mitchell knew the commissioner was not opposed to initiative among the troops, but he still adjusted his strategy to French's standing orders. French was aware that the clouds of dust the men and animals kicked up made riding anywhere but at the front of the column uncomfortable. With their welfare in mind, he rotated the lead troop so that all troopers might eat their share of dust. But Mitchell had discovered that a prepared troop could easily fall into second place in the line, where the dust was a hell of a lot less than at the rear.

Mitchell woke his men earlier than usual on this day. The Métis had informed him of a nearby watering hole, St. Peter's Spring. It had been days since the men had enjoyed a refreshing drink. They had hoped to find water at Rivière des Lacs, but found only dried-out remnants. It wasn't surprising. The unbearable heat sucked the earth dry. Mitchell figured that an early departure would allow his troop to escape traveling during the worst heat and give them early access to the clear water of the spring.

Given the reward, the men enthusiastically prepared to move out. And while they tried to be quiet about it, they discovered that there simply was no such thing as silence when breaking camp.

"Cripes!" came a surprised cry, followed immediately by a thud. "Who tied the goddamn guide rope to the cart?" A sub-constable picked himself up off the ground.

The angry words startled Sam Steele awake. The men were up and about? Had he missed the trumpet call of reveille? Horrified at the possibility, he dressed quickly and leaped from his tent still buttoning his pants.

As his eyes adjusted to the predawn light, he discovered that only part of the camp was active. Bewilderment gave way to relief when he heard the reassuring peal of the trumpet. Steele made his way to Mitchell.

"J.B., what's going on here? You're aware it's our turn to ride at the fore?"

"Just decided to get an early start on the day, Sam."

"There's nothing under the sun or the stars that'll get these men to move out early. Not just to get an early start. What do you know?" demanded Steele.

"Between me and you, Sam, there's a watering hole not too far off. Lévéillé told me as much. Get your men ready to go. We won't leave it too muddy for you!"

Steele was upset that he had been scooped on the information about the spring, but he took Mitchell's advice as a challenge. With Herculean effort, he spurred his men into action. Although E Troop had the head-start advantage, Steele had fine-tuned the workings of A Troop. They watched him pack gear like a man possessed and quickly fell into step with him. Their efforts increased as the rumor of fresh water on the horizon trickled from man to man. Not surprisingly, given Steele's leadership, A Troop was ready to move out at the head of the line.

A Troop set off at 3:30. After hours of difficult marching, they were met with shoulder-breaking disappointment. St. Peter's Spring was a dirty mud hole.

"There's water here men, but it won't be easy to get. Let's break out the shovels and dig some wells." Steele himself led the assault on the thick brown stew.

Eventually, after placing some half barrels bored with holes at the base of the wells, the water was clear enough to drink and quenched the thirst of 300 horses. And the men got enough to remind them what a drink was like. As he rode off later that afternoon, all Fred Bagley could think about was the

Henri Julien's drawing of the NWMP at mysterious La Roche Percée, July 1874

great disservice done to the apostle by the man who had christened the spring with his name.

Fortunately, conditions were about to change. La Roche Percée came into view by mid-afternoon. The unmistakable sandstone arch rose 35 feet into the air with a tail of tall, receding columns that stretched along about 140 feet. The sight raised flagging spirits because the men knew that Short Creek, a tributary of the Souris River, lay just beyond the marker. When they arrived, they were not disappointed. Water, wood and grass were abundant.

Rumors had it that Sub-Inspector Albert Shurtliff, whom French had detailed with 10 men to the northerly post of Fort Ellice in May, would join the force with fresh horses and extra supplies. Everyone hoped the rumors were true.

Day 18, Short Creek, near La Roche Percée
Rest Day

On July 25, while the men camped on the Short Creek near La Roche Percée, French decided to break up the force. He had been evaluating the pros and cons of such a move for days. Ultimately, however, the speed at which the force was traveling determined his decision. There was simply no way that they could reach the Bow River, establish a post, dispatch men to Fort Edmonton and return east with the remainder by Christmas. French decided to continue on with only the main body of the force and the necessary supplies and equipment. He'd send the rest to Fort Ellice and Fort Edmonton.

But plans to divide the force were temporarily forgotten when two officers arrived. The force's assistant surgeon, Dr. Richard Nevitt, rode in from Fort Dufferin. He had started out on the march on July 8 but had to return to accompany two ill men, both well past the point of continuing on without irreparable harm to their health. On his return, he brought a bag of letters, so welcomed by the men that even those who failed to receive one had their spirits uplifted. All were shocked, however, at the troubling news Nevitt brought. Reports in eastern Canada announced the tragic loss of the force—wiped out by hostile Sioux!

The reports had apparently filtered north from American newspapers. French immediately concluded that the source of the malicious stories were the disgruntled deserters, and while he could do little about them, he could at least calm frazzled nerves back in Ottawa. He wrote a hurried report underlining their inaccuracy and dispatched a trooper east with it. At least he could deal with that problem. The predicament posed by the second arrival left him throwing his hands in the air.

In early May, before the force's departure from Fort Dufferin, French had detailed Sub-Inspector Albert Shurtliff to take 10 men to Fort Ellice and establish the first of the force's detachments at what would serve as the North-West Mounted Police's headquarters. Shurtliff's responsibilities included checking cart traffic on the old Hudson's Bay Company trail between Fort Garry and Fort Edmonton for illicit booze and preparing for the arrival of the force when it eventually made its way back from the West. But French also intended to draw upon Shurtliff's supplies to replenish the main body's stocks, a prescient decision given what French considered the quartermaster's poor efforts to properly supply the force. French had directed the sub-inspector to meet the force at La Roche Percée with food and horses.

French was shocked when the sub-inspector arrived with only six horses. Shurtliff protested that the supply stock in Fort Ellice had become so precariously low that he felt he had no alternative but to send men and horses back to Fort Garry for additional goods. French had counted on the animals, and no excuse could satisfy him. Shurtliff found himself subject to a tongue lashing only known and perfected in military circles.

Shurtliff did bring food, a cartload of pemmican that French ordered dispersed immediately. Many of the men had never tasted this staple of the plains, and the pounded dried meat and marrow was a welcome change from their sailor's diet. When Henri Julien declared the pemmican delicious, he must have spoken for many because by day's end, the pemmican cart was available to carry something else. James Macleod could only wonder how much less burdensome the journey could have been had the commissioner decided to take an extra 10,000 pounds of pemmican instead of two nine-pound guns. He also wondered why French hadn't made better preparations to ensure the availability of fresh horses.

In fact, the assistant commissioner had begun questioning many of French's decisions, although he rarely took his concerns to his superior. Over the past month, his suspicions about French's ability to command were sharpened. The commissioner continued to be inept at delegating authority. He did not include Macleod in crucial command decisions and usually rejected his delicate suggestions. He also considered the commissioner excessively harsh on the men, pushing them too hard on too little sustenance and expecting them not to complain. Macleod's suggestion that they weren't soldiers went unheeded, and other sympathetic attempts to ease the burden on men or animals were generally met with derision.

Resigned to his fate, Macleod went back to gnawing on his pemmican.

Day 20, Short Creek, near La Roche Percée
Rest Day

Anxious to explore La Roche Percée, Fred Bagley was happy to be relieved of his job of dividing and reloading the force's supplies. The great natural monument was a place of mystery. He listened intently as the Métis described the giant cavern that yawned beneath the odd formation and how it served as a place of sanctuary and escape for Natives. Search as he might for a passage to the magical subterranean safe haven, Bagley couldn't find it. But he was not disappointed. Scratched into the sandstone of the outcropping were drawings that clearly originated in prehistoric times. Bagley dreamed of the noble Natives who had stood where he planted his feet. Nothing, however, matched the excitement of discovering the name of General George Armstrong Custer! Bagley traced his finger along the inscription and felt he was one with the great commander of the Seventh Cavalry.

Having fully explored La Roche Percée, Bagley made his way back to camp. Perhaps he'd be lucky enough to get a turn with one of the rifles the commissioner had ordered distributed. Unfortunately, each troop received only one rifle. Bagley could understand the reasoning behind the short supply. He'd witnessed some fool accidentally shoot a horse at far range and nearly cause a stampede! More than a month had passed since the violent thunderstorm at Fort Dufferin, and the horses still shied at loud noises. Bagley could understand it, but he didn't like it. One rifle took a long time to work its way through the men of B Troop, all of whom claimed to be excellent hunters, although they returned with little food. The troop bugler was far down the list.

Bagley contented himself with thoughts of evening revelries. The men had taken to creating their own form of campfire recreation. Under a cover of stars that awed even the seasoned veterans, the quiet prairie night was shattered as good voices and bad joined Constable Latimer and his fife, and Constable Parks with his tin plate and tent pegs. *Tenting in the Old Campground* and other songs of home drifted across the plains. Bagley tried to contribute by blowing a few notes on the bugle, but he was told to knock it off. It reminded too many of reveille. The stories and jokes gave Bagley the feeling that a real esprit de corps had finally developed among the men. He hadn't seen any Natives yet, but the march was beginning to approximate the adventure he had hoped for when he signed on.

Day 22, Wood End Depot
9.25 Miles Traveled

At lunchtime on Wednesday, July 29, French heaved a sigh of relief. Since Monday morning he had spent most of his time supervising the work of dividing stores into a Supply

Force and a Fighting Force, and the work was finally completed. He put Inspector William Jarvis of A Troop in command of the Supply Force. French had considered sending Macleod, but despite his penchant for unseemly comradery with the men and weak discipline, the commissioner viewed him as too valuable a liaison between command and the troopers. If only Macleod knew!

French directed Jarvis to accompany Sub-Inspector Shurtliff's party of seven to Fort Ellice and then continue on to Fort Edmonton via the Fort Garry–Fort Edmonton Trail. Included in the Supply Force were 12 men from A Troop, 12 Métis and the quartermaster. They took 55 of the weakest horses, 24 wagons, 55 carts, 62 oxen, 50 cows and calves and nonessential supplies, including agricultural implements and 25,000 pounds of the seemingly limitless supply of flour. Six sick men would also travel to Fort Ellice.

James Macleod looked at the provisions marked for going north and shuddered. He couldn't find fault with the commissioner's decision to rid the main body of items that slowed its progress. But they still had many miles to cover, and Jarvis' load of superfluous supplies might mean the difference between making it and starving. He was especially concerned about the new direction the force would be taking—northwest, away from the Boundary Commission Road. French had informed Macleod that Ottawa had ordered the change. Officials believed it prudent to steer clear of possible Sioux encounters near the border. Still, it also meant traveling away from the Boundary Commission camps, which could serve as key supply depots if food ran short. He kept his concerns to himself.

French ordered the men to remain camped at Wood End Depot until Friday. He was aware that there would be little fuel along the trail for the next week, and he wanted the men to cook rations and collect enough wood for an extended period.

Day 25, Long River
28 Miles Traveled

By August 1, the flat, barren land was having an undue effect on Henri Julien. The monotonous terrain proved mentally exhausting, and when conversation waned, he found the heavy blanket of silence increasingly oppressive. Since they had left La Roche Percée, even the elements conspired against them; it was hot and still, without so much as a refreshing breeze. When the force halted to rest in the afternoon, Julien, eager for a change, set out with a Métis guide in search of duck. They separated near a pond, and while Julien had a rifle, he was a poor marksman and did not expect success. Surprising even himself, his first shot hit the mark.

Julien set out to retrieve his kill because it had fallen into a slough. He dismounted and walked to the water's edge, leading his mustang Old Rooster by the bridle. When he reached it, he let the bridle slip from his hand and stepped into the water. Just as he had the duck in his hand, Old Rooster bolted straight away from camp.

"Sacré bleu! Why didn't I tie him up?" muttered Julien. "Old Rooster!" he called in vain. "Whoa, boy!" Disgusted, Julien threw down the duck and raced after the animal.

Julien soon caught up with the horse, but Old Rooster wouldn't let him catch hold of the bridle. With each attempt, the animal showed a sudden and uncharacteristic burst of speed and darted away. This two-step continued for nearly 10 miles, and with each mile, Julien grew increasingly convinced that the animal was purposely teasing him. In response, he let loose a barrage of colorful insults that would have shocked his hard-edged newspaper friends back east. All without effect, however. Obviously, capture would require strategy.

The illustrator maneuvered himself in front of the horse and spoke to it in more civilized and loving tones.

"Old Rooster, haven't I been good to you? Don't you get good rubdowns and plenty of water? You know I look out for you. Sure, I care more for you than I do myself.

"Listen. It's time I let out my secret. All this time, I've been keeping a few cubes of sugar. They're yours. Just imagine that sweet taste on your tongue." He licked his lips in exaggeration for emphasis.

"What is it, boy? Don't like the name Old Rooster? Of course, you're not old. I should never have called you that. It was a bad joke. I agree. From now on, just Rooster. How about it?" he begged.

It seemed to work. The horse settled down, and Julien lunged for the bridle. Success! Julien mounted the now-placid animal.

"You will be waiting a long time before you get any sugar from me, *Old* Rooster, you bastard."

Julien rode back to camp, and reflected on recent events.

"Maybe I was a bit too hard on you, boy. After all, what can one expect from a half-wild beast bred to the Plains." He whacked the animal on the neck. "When we get back, you'll get your sugar."

But when they got back, there was no sugar to be had. The force was long departed! Julien found their tracks and set off after them, but as the shadows lengthened, he could see no sign of the men. Tired, Julien felt it best to abandon his search until the next day. To prevent the horse's escape, he tied the animal's bridle to its pastern. Using his hard saddle as a pillow, the weary and hungry Julien forced all thoughts of disaster out of his mind and quickly fell asleep.

His eyes weren't closed long before he awoke to the prairie plague—mosquitoes. They sought him out like bloodhounds. With only the hopelessly inadequate protection of a few handkerchiefs, Julien was at their mercy, but he was so tired that even their attack couldn't deprive him of sleep.

Commissioner French, meanwhile, was busy until late Saturday night, writing the reports, which seemed to occupy much of his time. One of the sub-constables interrupted him.

"Sir, beggin' your pardon, but one of the men's missin'.'"

"So, what else is new," French muttered to himself. "Who is this time?"

"Julien, sir. The illustrator."

"Damn. Send up two rockets and make sure they're not too close to the horses. Ready the field gun for firing."

But Julien did not see or hear them.

Day 26, Long River
Rest Day

Julien awoke early, hardly refreshed but determined to find the camp. First he found that Old Rooster had broken loose. He could see him in the distance, but like the day before, the animal scooted off when he approached it.

"Goddamn it, you son of a bitch!" Julien had given up on bribes and bargaining. Old Rooster took him another six or seven miles away before Julien finally caught him. He was so tired that he rode the horse bareback back to the saddle.

Soon after sun-up, the search party stumbled upon him.

"Kittson!" cried Julien. "Thank God." Relieved Julien dismounted and fell into the doctor's arms.

"Dear God, man," said the astonished doctor. "You look terrible. Have you only been gone one day?"

Julien looked at his hands, raw, blistered and bleeding. His feet were little better, and he could only imagine his face.

"Western savages, Kittson."

"Sioux?"

"Mosquitoes."

When Julien returned to camp, the force had finished its regular Sunday church parade. As was the practice, the commissioner had taken the Church of England party while others

Henri Julien's drawing of an Evening Guard Parade, as it appeared in the *Canadian Illustrated News*, February 1875

~•⊃€⊂•~

gathered with the senior officer of each denomination. While French enjoyed the hymns, he lamented that the daily language of most men was far from scriptural. But his joy on this day was tempered by what lay ahead. This week the force would head northwest as per directions from Ottawa, away from the Boundary Commission Road, which turned south into the United States. For the past four weeks, French had depended on a rough map of the Boundary Commission Road, but it would be useless on the new route. He also had a map, made during Palliser's exploratory expedition in the late 1850s, but it had already proved inaccurate. French would have been less concerned had the guides proven their worth, but sadly, they lacked ability and continued to demonstrate a most irritatingly lackadaisical idea of a day's work. Even their knowledge of the terrain was questionable. French questioned them on certain distances, the correct answers to which he knew. One of the men failed miserably, proving himself an imposter.

French believed the lieutenant-governor had let him down in his recommendation of guides, and he was not sure what to do.

Day 28, Approximately 360 Miles West of Fort Dufferin
20 Miles Traveled

The day started earlier than usual, when a thunderstorm woke the men just after midnight. The accompanying winds blew down most of the tents. French worried the horses would stampede, and once found, would then need recovery time. If the force was to reach the Bow and Belly Rivers before winter, they would have to avoid unnecessary delays. His greatest fear materialized when the horses spooked, and two groups stampeded. Fortunately, the pickets the men set up stopped them from running far. And the men caught a few hours sleep after they re-pegged their tents. They marched at 7:00 AM.

Sub-Inspector Cecil Denny, the son of an English aristocrat, rode along at the end of the column. He had been assigned rear-guard duty, although there was little threat to guard against. It was a punishment for his thoughtless action the previous day.

Even Denny admitted he'd made a fine ass of himself. Sub-Inspectors McIllree and French had made a great discovery. Antelope! After untold meals of dried goods, the anticipation of fresh venison had the men salivating. Denny tagged along as the officers stealthily made their way towards the herd. They had just come within firing range when Denny, unable to resist participating in the kill, broke ranks and ran towards the previously oblivious antelope. The animals scattered and were still running hard when they disappeared from view.

French had a mind to unload his shot in Denny's rear end, and was only just convinced by Sub-Inspector McIllree not to do so. Shamefaced, Denny returned to camp. He was already the butt of many cruel jokes, since few men believed his unending litany of stories about his American adventures. They had begun to call him "Texas Jack" more in mockery than in respect. The antelope escapade merely confirmed in the minds of many that the young Englishman was really just a tenderfoot.

Denny seethed as he stomped along, oblivious to all but the horizon. Suddenly, he saw something move. By God, it was an antelope! Well, he'd show everyone. He'd take down that animal, and there'd be fresh meat tonight. No one would doubt "Texas Jack" anymore.

Denny slipped away towards the animal unnoticed, imagining his triumphant return. He pictured himself throwing the antelope at the feet of French and McIllree. "Here, boys," he'd say. "It's on me!" He swung wide as he rode, hoping to stay downwind of the animal. He kept his eyes fixed on his prey, unwilling to risk losing it. Not much farther to go, just a couple of hundred yards.

Suddenly, his horse stopped moving, and the horizon began to rise. He was sinking!

Within seconds, the sucking mud reached his horse's belly. Denny scrambled, kicked his feet free from the stirrups and thrashed about trying to grab for solid ground. When he found it, he lay still, heart racing and breathing in rapid pants. Then he watched his horse continue to sink. It stopped with only its head poking out of the quicksand.

Denny stretched out and grabbed for the bridle. It was almost within reach...just a little more...and then he had it. He pulled hard, but the horse couldn't budge. Denny saw the terror in the animal's glossy bulging eyes, but he was powerless to help.

He stood up. He'd need help. He looked in the direction of the force. Nothing. In a panic, he scanned the horizon. It was empty. Not even a sign of dust.

"Settle down, Cecil," he muttered to himself. "Think about this. You can figure it out."

Denny knew that if he didn't find the force, he'd die. A man adrift on the plains was without hope. He looked up at the sun to determine the direction of his trail and finally settled on a course. He walked for hours. His lips began to crack, and his feet blistered and bled. He took off his tattered jacket and wrapped it around his head since he'd lost his helmet in the quicksand. It proved poor protection against the unforgiving sun. It wouldn't be a worry much longer, since it was already well into its descent. Would night be any better? His thoughts quickly turned to wolves. Hungry, bloodthirsty and savage.

Then he saw something moving! Were his eyes playing tricks on him? Was it an apparition? No. It looked like a man on a horse! Denny ran towards him. Close enough to determine that it wasn't a Native, he shouted, a hoarse croak. Again he called, this time with better results. The man heard him! He turned and rode towards him!

"Major Macleod," he whimpered, falling at the feet of the assistant commissioner's horse. "Thank you, Lord!"

"I'm guessing you could use some assistance, Denny?" Macleod had been dispatched by Commissioner French to return to the Wood Mountain Depot for pemmican because supplies would be difficult to acquire along the new route. Macleod had ridden ahead of the transport carts in search of bogged-down wagons.

Denny blurted out the whole story.

"I marked where it happened, sir, but I'm not sure I can find it again."

Macleod had two horses and handed Denny the reins of his spare animal.

"Horses are too valuable to abandon. Let's take a look."

The pair came upon the trapped horse after about an hour. Miraculously, it was still alive.

Macleod slung his lasso around the horse's head. He tied the other end to his saddle horn. Together the men and the horses heaved as they struggled to pull the animal free. Exhausted from fear and the pressure of the quicksand on its body, the trapped horse could not move. But slowly, the rescuers' efforts raised the animal a few inches. Once the horse sensed the possibility of freedom, it began to kick wildly, and soon it escaped the quicksand. It fell to the ground and lay still, its chest slowly rising and falling.

They gave the animal time to regain its strength, and then coaxed it to its feet. They returned to the carts, and Macleod pointed Denny in the direction of the force.

"It's only a few miles northwest," he said. As Denny turned to ride away, Macleod added, "Antelope really shouldn't be your prey of choice."

Day 32, Old Wives Lakes
30.5 Miles Traveled

Early on Saturday, August 8, the force descended from the Dirt Hills plateau to a welcome change in terrain. On Friday, French had given the order for a day's rest to allow the horses to recover from the exhausting ascent. He also decided to ignore the advice of the guides because their incompetence so threatened the success of the march. His training as an artillery officer and gunner included an education in surveying techniques, and he decided to use his skills to guide the force. But it was laborious work, requiring him to take angles at every turn of the route. At the noon halt, when most others made up for the sleep they were deprived of by early starts, he took the altitude of the sun to discover the force's latitude. French became a regular nightly sight to those few awake after midnight, his eyes trained on the heavens to obtain the magnetic variation by Polestar. He used the figures to plot out the route and marked it on Palliser's Map.

For the better part of the day, the column snaked west along an old trail. It made for an easy march allowing many miles to be covered.

Late in the afternoon, the men sighted a lake in the distance. French noted that the lake was a good 20 miles east of its location on Palliser's map. Hardly encouraging. The men were less concerned about the route than the enjoyment that awaited. Thoughts of the pleasures experienced at the Souris River danced in their heads. Fred Bagley shared in the excitement. He was walking alongside his cart when he saw the lake and called back to the Métis driver behind him to inform him.

"Ah, *oui*," replied Cardinal. "This Old Wives Lakes."

"Odd name," said Bagley.

"It has a sad story, my boy."

"Can you tell it to me?" asked the ever-enthusiastic Bagley.

The Métis was silent for a moment and then spoke.

"I tell the story of Old Wives Lakes with great respect for the women it was named for," he began.

"Many springs ago, a great fire swept across the prairies. It left the land black, and the buffalo, they not come. The Cree from the east of Wood Mountain are hungry after the long winter. They need to eat the buffalo. So they go west, farther than they ever did before. They know it is the home of their enemy, the Blackfoot, but without the buffalo, they not survive.

"Along the shores of this lake, the Cree find the great beasts. They kill many. Many old women on this hunt. Their skills

Less than two weeks into the march Commissioner French wrote in his diary, "Horses very weak." As depicted here in Henri Julien's drawing, the NWMP crossed the Dirt Hills three weeks later. French had long since issued the order that the men march to ease the horses' burden. French finally realized that appearance was less important than function, admitting that the eastern thoroughbreds "having been purchased more for the saddle than draught, ran rapidly down in condition when placed at such work." The spirits of the men also sagged, and many grumbled as they pulled the artillery and marched in a supposedly mounted force. After conquering the five-mile, 1000-foot climb of the Dirt Hills, French camped to allow the horses to rest. The progress of the march was increasingly dictated by the animals' condition.

were needed to make pemmican. Soon the ponies were loaded down with pemmican. As they turn to ride back east, the Blackfoot strike. On their fast war ponies, they ride into camp, hanging on their ponies' sides like the Comanche. Two Cree are killed and many more injured," said Cardinal.

"The Cree knew they are safe for the night because the cowardly Blackfoot not attack in the dark. The Cree powwow to come up with a plan. The chiefs know that they no get home with the load of pemmican. All they could do was leave it. But they couldn't because everyone would starve. Then one of the old women, she ask to speak.

"'We have seen many summers. We can no longer have sons to fight as braves. You return to our people with the pemmican. Go in the dark. We stay. Build many small fires, talk loud and make the Blackfoot think that all are still camped here.'

"That's just what those Cree do. When Blackfoot attack next day, they find only the gray-haired women. Angry, they torture and kill them, but gray scalps not a thing to be proud of. Blackfoot not care," he spat.

"Even today, when Indians come here, they keep clear of Old Wives Lakes. They are afraid of ghosts." Cardinal made the sign of the cross.

The force arrived at the eastern lake of Old Wives Lakes (Lake Johnston) near midnight. They found immense flocks of wildfowl, and although tired, the men had enough energy to hunt and cook. They ate well, but were unable to quench their thirst with the brackish and alkaline lake water.

CHAPTER SIX

From Old Wives Lakes to the Cypress Hills

Day 34, Old Wives Lakes
6.5 Miles Traveled
EDWARD MAUNSELL ALSO HEARD the story of Old Wives Lakes, but he looked upon the tale with suspicion. After one night camped on its shore, he was convinced that another powerful force kept the Métis and Natives away—lice.

They infested the camp and terrorized man and animal alike. Maunsell suspected that Natives long since gone had brought the cooties because he heard that the pests could survive at an abandoned camp forever. Old Wives Lakes proved the rumor true. Nothing he had ever experienced prepared him for the misery they caused.

And, of course, the cooties were worse during the night, when the exhausted men sought their much-needed sleep. As soon as their heads hit the ground, the torment began, and for a man like Maunsell who enjoyed his rest, the situation proved simply unbearable. The gauntlet was thrown down, and Maunsell would meet the challenge. He washed his clothes with uncharacteristic vigor but discovered that it had no impact on the creatures. Once dried and dressed, his desperate scratching began anew. He turned to Dr. Kittson, but the mercurial ointment he provided was only mildly effective.

Maunsell would have to be more cunning and study his opponent in preparation for his attack. After some observation, he noticed the lice were slow-moving creatures. It struck him that if he removed his shirt and turned it inside out, it might take the cooties some time to make their way back inside. He tried it that night, and for his efforts was granted a good night's sleep. Maunsell's solution gave him a measure of notoriety in the camp, and for the following few days, officer and trooper alike blessed his name.

French would have preferred to give the men and horses another day's rest at Old Wives Lakes, but the water was brackish and the feed poor, so they marched about six miles along the lake's southern shore until the feed improved.

That day wasn't without its highlight, however. In mid-afternoon, Macleod rejoined the force. His supply team carried 4700 pounds of pemmican and dried meat, and the force met them with unreserved glee. The supplies came none too soon. The men's meals had been reduced to biscuits and porridge (although the horses got most of the oats), while the officers were down to a cut ration of bacon. Macleod was practically a hero.

Day 36, Old Wives Creek
5 Miles Traveled

Wednesday, August 12 was a long day. A hill with an impassable slope impeded the march. French ordered the advance guard to cut it down to a reasonable slope, drastically limiting the day's advance. But the evening's excitement made the men forget about the day's poor progress.

Fred Bagley ran through the camp towards the commissioner's tent, undeterred by the obstacle course of equipment, leaping over objects like a jackrabbit. He had no time to waste. A Sioux was in camp!

Bagley saw the brave as the man left French's tent. The Native wasn't as tall as he expected, but the bare-breasted and bronzed warrior was nonetheless a fine specimen. His shiny, braided black hair extended far past his shoulder blades. He wore leather leggings tooled with beadwork that matched the design on his moccasins. He slipped onto his pony and, with a ramrod straight back, rode bareback out of camp.

Yes, thought Bagley, *finally a brave whose type filled the pages of Cooper.*

Bagley spied Julien nearby.

"Henri, did you see him?"

"*Mais oui*. Although I got to say he wasn't much to see," replied Julien.

"Oh, come on Henri. He was a real brave!"

"Yeah, but he was dirty and ugly. He had a low, protruding brow and looked like a brute. If the women are anything like him, there's either a lot of single or very desperate men."

"Is he camped nearby?" asked Bagley, ignoring the slight.

"About three-quarters of a mile away, I hear. With seven tipis and about 30 of his kin."

"Want to go look?" pleaded Bagley.

"No need. They're coming back tomorrow for a powwow."

Fred Bagley could hardly sleep that night.

Day 37, Old Wives Creek
Rest Day

French was up early, giving directions in preparation for the Natives' arrival. He had learned that they were Sisseton Sioux, refugees from the violence in Minnesota in the early 1860s. Like Julien, the commissioner saw them as poor specimens of either physical prowess or dignified nobility. But they were the first Natives the force had encountered, and French

Henri Julien's drawing of the first Sioux encountered on the march. It appeared in the *Canadian Illustrated News* April 1875.

~⊃X⊂~

thought it important that they be treated with respect and honesty. Who knew how far the stories of this powwow might travel? French considered it best to assume they might reach deep into Blackfoot territory, and so it was important that he address the leader of these poor folks as if he was talking to a great chief.

The Sioux arrived early, but French made them wait for the appointed hour. They sat outside camp until word came from

Lévéillé, the designated interpreter for the occasion. Lévéillé could not speak Sioux, but fortunately one of the Natives was fluent in Cree.

"The chief of the Red Coats is now ready to powwow with the red children of the Great White Mother [Queen Victoria], who lives across the big waters."

The brave who was apparently the chief of the group nodded and organized his party. The Sioux arranged themselves in a line, with the men before the women. The chief stood at the fore, holding high in his right hand what appeared to be an symbol of his position, an object made of fur, feather and bone. As the Natives marched into the camp, they uttered a monotone chant. Peals of trumpets signaling the camp's welcome soon drowned out their chanting. Everyone fell silent when the group reached the pavilion, two large tents linked together, specifically set up for the meeting.

An officer escorted the chief to French, who, resplendent in full dress uniform, exuded unquestioned authority. His officers, similarly dressed, surrounded him. The previous night their batmen, sub-constables assigned to perform the more menial duties of servants, had been busy ridding clothing of dust and dirt, and the result was impressive.

The chief stood before the commissioner, and after Lévéillé translated introductions, French invited the Sioux to sit down. The braves positioned themselves on the ground on one side of the tent, while their women squatted opposite them. French sat behind a table, while his officers arranged themselves on makeshift benches or on the ground. Once settled, the chief took out his long-stemmed pipe, a beautiful instrument made of red stone inlaid with silver and quite possibly the band's most valuable possession. The chief gave it to one of his men to fill with kinnic-kinnic (an aromatic herb) and tobacco. He lit it and passed the pipe around those gathered, with braves and officers taking deep drags. French took only a quick puff, which he quickly exhaled. The concerned chief looked to Lévéillé, who explained that the commissioner did not smoke. The Natives looked confused.

French nodded to one of his officers, the signal to distribute presents. The officer retrieved a bag and went to the center of the pavilion. One of the braves stepped forward to receive a 10-pound bag of black plug tobacco. He took it back to the chief.

With that, one of the Sioux stood. He walked over to the officers and shook their hands. Then he spoke. He talked for some time, and the wide-eyed officers sat captivated. While they didn't understand a word he said, they stared at his arm movements and his facial expressions, which revealed as much as his speech. When he was finished, he again shook hands with the officers and retreated to his position on the floor. Lévéillé began his interpretation.

Why is it that those with hair on their faces are rich? We have no hair on our chins and are poor. Many moons ago, we were on the other side of the Medicine Line [international boundary]. *We had horses and land. We wanted for nothing. Then the Wasichus* [white men] *come. They lie and take our land. They give us drink and kill us with their guns. We wished to live in peace but could not. The Wasichus forced us across the Medicine Line to the land of the Great White Mother.*

We are happy here where the Great White Mother protects us. She does not allow so many bad things to happen to her red children. We live in peace. But we are hungry. We need rifles and bullets to hunt the buffalo. We need them for protection when we meet the Wasichus.

We heard you were coming. We know you will help us. Are you not here to do that? We will help you. Our children will help you. I tell no lies.

Commissioner French rose to speak. He directed Lévéillé to translate as he did.

My red brothers want to know why we come. The Great White Mother has heard that bad Americans are selling you whiskey and that it makes you sick. She does not want you to be sick. She loves her children, regardless of their color. She has sent us to punish the whiskey traders and anyone who helps them.

This elicited an excited reply from the Sioux.

We have traveled for a month and will travel one more month to where the bad people are. We will capture those who hurt the Great White Mother's red children. We do not want the land of the Sioux nor the land of the Great White Mother's red children.

The news was apparently welcome, greeted by a chorus of enthusiastic grunts.

Our guns are only for our warriors, but we have other presents for you. Calico, tea and ammunition. The ammunition is only to be used for hunting.

A designated officer brought in the presents and supplemented them with some flour and flints. Once they were distributed, another brave rose to speak. Again Lévéillé translated when the brave fell silent.

Many moons ago, my chief said that Wasichus would come to help us. I did not believe it. Wasichus come only to hurt. Now you are here, and I believe it. I have never seen Wasichus like you before. I will be kind as you are. Give us bullets and guns and we will help you. Last year the son of our chief died like so many of our bravest warriors. Before he died he told me to stay in this land of the Great White Mother. Today I am glad I did. I will help as I can. I am not a great chief. I am only a warrior who likes to speak, though like a child, I cannot do it well.

Once Lévéillé finished, the pipe made the rounds of the tent again. As they stood to leave, the chief spoke.

"We thank the Great White Mother and Wachasta Sota."

Lévéillé later informed French that the name "Wachasta Sota" referred to him, the "man with power."

With that, the powwow was complete. The Sioux departed and made their way back to their nearby camp.

Day 38, Old Wives Creek
Rest Day

Fred Bagley had been one of the many troopers who struggled to catch a glimpse of the powwow through the opening of the pavilion. As one of the smaller men, his elbows proved inadequate for the task. Disappointed, he thought he had missed his first opportunity to see the western Natives up close. He need not have worried. The Sioux soon returned and danced for the camp.

Bagley stood enraptured as the Sioux gathered in a circle and sang. He had no idea what the song meant, but imagined it was a story of long ago heroic exploits or future daring adventures. As they sang, they hopped and shuffled from one foot to the other. Slowly, they moved clockwise, eventually retracing their steps. It was an odd dance, foreign to Bagley's experience, which made it all the more captivating. He joined in a round of applause when they finished but didn't have the courage to join the handful of his comrades who danced their own jig. Bagley noted that the Sioux seemed insulted by the impromptu response, and they quickly departed.

The Sioux returned later, and by sundown, they were treating the camp as if it was their own. Troopers found them in their tents, planted as firmly as oak trees, unwilling to move. They came to trade and, since the troopers wanted the souvenirs, the few possessions of the Sioux brought them quick returns. One lucky man procured a scalp. Fred Bagley nearly died from disappointment when he heard that. He had to get something, but he had little to trade. Fleetingly, he thought of his bugle; he could claim it was lost or stolen. However, the consequences of his ruse being discovered were too great because he'd already been placed on report once for misplacing it. Instead, he scrounged up some buttons and tobacco and managed to trade for some moccasins. They'd come in handy since Bagley's riding boots were held together with rawhide straps.

Day 40, Old Wives Creek
Rest Day

Commissioner French's batman stepped into his tent and informed him that the Métis guides wished a conference.

"Very well," sighed French. "Send them in."

Lévéillé, Morin and a man unknown to French entered.

"French," began Lévéillé, who, like most of the Métis, did not use proper titles, "we are in strange territory. None of us have been this far west. We know not what lies ahead."

And your knowledge of where we've been was hardly thorough, thought French. *At least you're finally being honest.*

"So, where does that leave us?" asked French.

"'Tis our good fortune that Francis Morriseau has arrived." Lévéillé pointed to the new man. "He knows this country very well."

French looked at the man. Little distinguished him from the other Métis save for a unkempt beard that was fuller than most. The beard, his long black hair, and a fringed buckskin jacket gave him a disheveled appearance. He wore leather pants and a multicolored sash tied around his waist. Because all the Métis wore such a sash, French assumed it must be part of their uniform.

"You're familiar with the territory?" asked French.

"I am from the Yankee Fort Benton. I have traveled north to Fort Edmonton, and I have hunted and traded in that country. I have also trapped on the Bow River three years ago."

French nodded. "Then you can tell me the location of the Belly River?"

"About halfway between Benton and Edmonton. Perhaps a little south of that."

About right, based on what I know, thought French. "I must say, given the knowledge of our current guides, your arrival is quite fortuitous. Why would you be out here alone?"

"Hunting," Morriseau replied.

"Really! We haven't seen a wild beast in days."

"The hunting has not been good."

"Indeed. What can you tell me about what lies west?"

"The Blackfoot are on the warpath. They have killed white traders, tortured one to death. They tied him to a tree and cut him many times."

French reflected on what Morriseau said. The previous day, an eastbound party of Métis hunters and traders had arrived at the camp, but they had not mentioned violence. They were traveling to Winnipeg with a supply of buffalo robes and had been stopped and their carts inspected for liquor. No contraband was found. If the party had been trading booze, they'd hardly be taking it back east. The traders had informed French that a large gathering of Métis and Natives was camped about

During the march the NWMP encountered the occasional party of Métis traders.

~❦~

four days' march away. But they were peaceful, merely awaiting the arrival of the buffalo.

As French surveyed Morriseau, he sensed something suspicious about him. Perhaps he was a spy for western liquor traders. Still, the fact remained that he seemed to know something of the territory that lay ahead, and such information was invaluable. French had finally seen the wisdom of Macleod's suggestion and begun sending out an advance guard each day, but the untrained troopers charged with searching for appropriate camping sites had not proved up to the task.

"Morriseau, I'll sign you on. You'll get the same pay as Léveillé and his men. If your skills do not match your professed ability, your employment will be short-lived. Come back tomorrow morning so we can plan the next leg of our journey."

Day 41, Old Wives Creek
Rest Day

French expected to move out from Old Wives Creek by this day. While the long layover had helped the men and animals, he doubted that more rest would be of much value. Only the continued absence of Assistant Commissioner Macleod, dispatched with 16 carts to the Boundary Commission post of Wood Mountain to obtain supplies three days earlier, kept the commissioner from giving the order to break camp. Macleod finally returned late in the day, but the slow moving carts of supplies, mostly some 60,000 pounds of oats, was well behind him. French thought the price Macleod paid was a trifle high, but he considered oats at any cost as a godsend to the horses.

Captain Lawrence Herchmer, a supply officer of the Boundary Commission and an acquaintance of French accompanied Macleod. His arrival was a welcome diversion for the commissioner. After an evening meal of greater substance than the troopers' current daily allowance of a half pound of bread, the pair sat in conversation. Small talk about mutual friends, Ottawa and the work of each man soon gave way to conditions in the West.

"Any trouble with the Indians?" asked French. "I've been told the Blackfoot are on the warpath."

"It's rare enough for us to see an Indian," replied Herchmer. "And when we do, they're in poor physical condition. Most commonly they stumble upon our camps and beg. They are hardly a threat. However, I was just down in Fort Benton, and the word there is that relations south of the border remain tense."

In 1872, Great Britain and the United States established a dual organization—Her Majesty's North American Boundary Commission and the United States Northern Boundary Commission—to mark the agreed-upon international boundary along the 49th parallel (1818 and 1846). The British (Canadian) contingent consisted of Royal Engineers, scouts and laborers. Surveying began in September 1872. While the Boundary Commissions were at work during the NWMP's march west, their activities in the eastern prairies were complete, and the force did not encounter them despite following the Boundary Commission road for 200 miles. Along the route, however, Boundary Commission depots provided rations and feed. This 1872 picture of the British (Canadian) Boundary Commission staff includes Lawrence Herchmer (back row, 4th from left) and David Cameron (front row, 3rd from left).

"Troubles there might cause problems here," reflected French. "I expect we'll see an increased number of Indian refugees in the future. And not just poor, but angry. Fortunately, those we have encountered have been a poor and motley lot. I expect that to change. Reports suggest it unlikely that the Blackfoot will be as docile or as dependent as the refugees."

"I agree. From what I've heard, they are fiercely independent. Unlike the northern Cree or some of the tribes to the east, they've long resisted bartering with the fur traders. The Blackfoot don't even want traders in their territory."

"Times are changing, Lawrence. The westward march of civilization will bring change whether the Blackfoot want it or not. From their perspective, the best they can hope for is an easy transition. It's the force's responsibility to help ensure it, and to do so we'll have to enter into Blackfoot territory and gain their confidence. An essential first step will be to remove the whiskey traders. Intelligence suggests that is where the troublesome element operates."

"Perhaps operated is a more accurate description. I understand from conversations in Fort Benton that few remain."

"Indeed?"

"Yes. I met with the Conrad brothers, fine gentlemen and proprietors of I.G. Baker, a substantial trading outfit that supplies much of the southwestern reaches of the North-West Territories. Be sure to look them up. I'm confident they can provide you with any supplies the force requires."

"I will," nodded French.

"The Conrads tell me their men have seen little illegal activity in the region. But if the rumors in Benton are true," added Herchmer, "the whiskey traders are determined to return across the border once the police force departs."

"No more than rumors?" asked French.

"Well, I haven't talked to any whiskey traders, George, but the opinion seems to be widely held."

"In that case it seems appropriate that the force establish a post in the region. I'll write a letter informing officials in Ottawa of the change. Would you telegraph it for me at your first opportunity?"

"Of course."

"I'll direct the reply to Fort Benton. I expect to be there in September."

"Remember to pack your sidearm when you're down there."

"Expect trouble, eh?"

"When folks talk about the Wild West, it's places like Benton they have in mind. It's full of wolfers, miners, whiskey traders, and other outlaws. It's a magnet for the lowest of the low in the northern territories. But there are also good men, like the Conrads."

"Meeting them will be a welcome change. This territory is large and barren, although I hardly need to tell you that."

"It can hardly be described to the uninitiated. The isolation is truly oppressing."

"And it poses significant problems. Confidentially, the march has been a challenge. As you're aware, supply problems have long plagued us. The men can take care of themselves, but it's been damn hard on the animals."

"So Macleod informed me. I saw some bony and fleshless horses penned up."

"What I wouldn't give for some fresh blood."

"I might be able to help you with that," replied Herchmer. "I brought a spare horse up from Wood Mountain. A damn good animal."

As a lover of fine horse flesh, French's interest grew with Herchmer's description. "Let's take a look at him."

It wasn't long before French owned the horse. And Herchmer promised that more horses would arrive with the carts. When the carts and horses finally rolled into camp, French was somewhat disappointed. These were the smallish Plains mustangs. Still he added five to the force's stock. He noticed that Macleod also bought one. Despite some reservations, French's approval of his assistant commander grew daily. While Macleod devoted too much energy to the men's comfort, which did not contribute to the mission's success, he was dependable. Yes, he was a good man for a second-in-command.

Day 43, Cripple Creek
14 Miles Traveled

The force finally broke camp, but French was less enthusiastic than he might have been. Since the arrival of Morriseau, the commissioner had long reflected on the Métis' comment about the Blackfoot on the warpath. Given what he had heard from the Métis trading party and Herchmer, he believed there was little truth to the information. Still, he couldn't be certain. More importantly, although he wouldn't admit it to anyone, there was no guarantee that the exhausted force could successfully repel a large-scale Native attack.

Also troubling was Morriseau's sudden disappearance. The day following his arrival, the scout left camp explaining that he needed to retrieve a cache of weapons he had left hidden near Wood Mountain. He informed his Métis friends when he expected to return, but that hour slipped by with no sign of the man. In response, French ordered Inspector Carvell and Acting Constable Latimer to travel to the southern post and arrest him. Just before they set out, Morriseau reappeared. French belayed the order, but his suspicion of the man's link to outlaws was reinforced. Careful observation showed no signs of any such men, but French knew that if they were out there, the outlaws' knowledge of the territory would give them a distinct advantage over the force.

In response to anticipated dangers, French decided to further trim the force. He culled seven men (five of them sick) and one Métis and placed them under the command of Sergeant

J. Sutherland. The party would rest and recover and await the part of the force that was to return east after the successful completion of their mission. Also left under Sutherland's charge were 28 of the most exhausted horses, some poor cattle, 14 wagons, a collection of stores not absolutely necessary and 20 days provisions for the returning troops. The men unceremoniously dubbed the depot Cripple Camp.

That night, with hostile Natives and outlaws in mind, French issued the men extra ammunition and posted a double guard to prevent any marauders from slipping in under cover of darkness.

Day 44, Old Wives Creek
21.5 Miles Traveled

"Goddamnit!" shouted Sub-Inspector John French, as he watched the horses of D Troop stampede under an assault of flying ants that had appeared when the force came upon Old Wives Creek again." Miles, get out here and help bring these horses under control!"

Sergeant Major T.W.S. Miles stumbled from his tent, pulling on a boot. Suspenders hanging low around his thighs, he barked orders. Within minutes the men were scattered among the horses on the moonlit plain. Following the stampedes of July, the horses had been carefully hoppled each night. The hopple was a piece of leather strung low around the horses' forelegs. The equipment proved effective, and since its use there'd not been any problems. On this night, they *were* properly hoppled, but as was discovered, the knee-haltering merely impeded the horses' ability to run; it could not stop a determined horse. And the flying ants gave the animals a steely determination.

The number of flying ants was insignificant compared to the great clouds of mosquitoes and grasshoppers that they had previously encountered, but in the pain they caused, they reigned supreme. Their bites were sharp and left throbbing red welts.

Later that night, and for all future nights, the horses were more securely tied up. Nevertheless, French remained concerned that a stampede might prove disastrous for the force.

Day 45, Approximately 513.5 Miles West of Fort Dufferin
25.5 Miles Traveled

On Friday, August 21, the commissioner's batman interrupted him with unexpected news.

"Sir, the men have discovered a strange party camping nearby in a field of cactus."

What could be stranger than where they've chosen to camp? thought French. "No mysteries, boy. What's strange about them?"

"Well, one's a trader, apparently the brother of the scout Lévéillé. With him are his two sons. But the other is a Roman Catholic priest."

"Indeed!" French rose from his chair. "Take me to them."

French met the men on the outskirts of the force's encampment and immediately identified the priest in his telltale flowing black robes. French stepped towards him.

"Commissioner George French, commander of the North-West Mounted Police." He extended his hand.

"Père Lestaing." The men shook hands.

"It is indeed a surprise to see a man of the cloth in these wilds," said French.

"Truly, the surprise is mine!" countered the priest in a thick French accent. "I have been in these parts for nearly 20 years. Never have I seen an armed force on this side of the border."

"We are new," agreed French and explained the nature and purpose of the force. "You are traveling to—?"

"Fort Edmonton."

"Ah. I have men traveling there myself. Perhaps you will meet with them on your journey."

"Possibly, although the land is, as I am sure you have discovered, large. And empty. Forgive me if I intrude, but if you are going to deal with the illegal traders near the Belly River, why are you so far north?"

"To avoid any possible encounter with hostile Sioux or Blackfoot, Père."

Lestaing's eyes surveyed the camp. Men were dressed in rags and wore haggard expressions. He could see why they might want to avoid any such encounter

"Père, we have a small number of Catholics among our numbers. Would you be willing to hear the confessions of those who so desire it? Perhaps even say a Mass?"

"Mais certainment." *And I will pray for the success of your mission*, thought Lestaing, *because only divine intervention will ensure that your men reach their destination.*

Day 46, Approximately 539 Miles West of Fort Dufferin
7.5 Miles Traveled

Saturday, August 22, started well enough with a refreshing rain shower, the first (save the thunderstorms) since the force had left Fort Dufferin. But it went downhill from there.

"There sure as hell hasn't been much action on this journey," complained Joseph Carscadden, an acerbic sub-constable with a critical eye directed usually at the commissioner. "A man is likely to see more in a brothel at noon."

"I'd like to know where all this booze is," said Maunsell. "We've stopped several Métis traders and not found a drop of liquor. Makes you wonder if this is a fool's errand."

"I don't know if it's a fool's errand," replied Carscadden, "but I don't think there's much doubt about the man who's leading us."

The men wondered in silence whether it was appropriate to continue the insubordinate line of discussion.

"I ask you," pushed Carscadden, "is there a man among us who didn't know that the horses chosen by French were not up to the job?"

"I guess there was one man."

"Yeah," snorted Carscadden. "The best that can be said for those eastern horses is that many of 'em weren't around long enough to continue their balky ways. But what gets me most is French's attitude towards the men. Everyone knows he cares more about the welfare of his own bloody horse than he does about his troopers. I'd hate to be his batman, forever tending to the beast. The emperor can't be seen riding on a horse that's not brushed to a fine glossy finish. My hair hasn't seen a comb since Dufferin," added Carscadden, as he dragged his fingers through his tangled mop. He thinks he's a goddamn king, and this is his fiefdom. Every time we stumble on a slough full of ducks, he starts firing. By the time any of us gets a crack, they're all frightened away, for God's sake."

"I heard he brought down 25 on the wing the other day."

"I'm not saying he's not a good shot, just a selfish one," replied Carscadden.

Perhaps French wasn't terribly concerned for the men's welfare, but he was worried about the horses. When he noticed the pasturage was increasingly cropped short, he conferred with the Métis guides. They informed him that the force had entered the eastern edge of the great buffalo range, and they predicted that little grass would be available for the horses west to the Rocky Mountains. French dispatched Macleod to a nearby Boundary Commission post at Frenchman's Creek on the White Mud River for supplies. Sub-Inspector James Walker, some troopers and 27 oxcarts with their Métis drivers accompanied him.

Day 49, Cypress Hills
14 Miles Traveled

There wasn't a trooper who didn't smile when the mind-numbing blandness of the prairie horizon finally gave way to the lush green Cypress Hills a few days earlier. Too long awash in the dull brown prairie, the men found the hills a feast for hungry eyes.

When the Cypress Hills came into sight, French immediately placed the men on high alert. Whiskey traders had been active in that region; the massacre in May of the previous year occurred just west of their current location. Of greater concern, however, were the Métis' warnings that the Cypress Hills were a well-known location of Native violence. Many tribes, including the Cree, Blackfoot, Blood and Sioux considered it valuable territory. They hunted and camped there, but over the years none had gained mastery over it. Continual warfare was the result.

French wasn't as concerned with inter-tribal warfare as he was with the troubling fact that the force had finally entered the eastern reaches of Blackfoot territory. And until he was certain the hostile tribe knew of the force's peaceful mission, he was determined to use caution. He ordered the men to don their scarlet tunics. He wanted no misunderstandings with the Blackfoot, no possibility that they might mistake the North-West Mounted Police for the American cavalry patrolling north of the boundary. So French issued a standing order that men would sleep fully dressed with rifles ready. Such preparedness might help prevent a catastrophe in case of ambush. He distributed extra ammunition, and added 30 men to the nightly guard to form a cordon around the camp. In addition, he charged the advance guard with carefully assessing the safety of the day's route.

Fred Bagley was assigned to the advance guard, a posting he greeted with mixed emotions. He had been terribly excited about the possibility of spying hostile braves—at a distance. But the early starting hour of the advance guard and the sheer demands of marching dampened his enthusiasm. He had heard that the trail they followed was named the Plain Hunters' Trail. In the past he might have thought such a route

carried romance and adventure, but that was a time long forgotten. Little dulled the imagination like physical exhaustion
tempered with constant repetition. His head lolled forward,
eyes hypnotized by the muddy expanse of trail directly before
him. The mud stuck like glue to his riding boots making each
step a burden. His thoughts drifted back to carefree days riding the cart, when he could even sneak a snack if he had the
urge. His raised his eyes and looked wistfully at the lancers
with their colorful pennants who rode alongside the advance
guard. The commissioner was taking careful measures to
impress those they might encounter.

Yesterday, the force had crossed the Rivière au Courant
(Swift Current River). Grading its high banks so the animals
and carts could successfully cross the river was hard work.
That night they camped in a valley in the Cypress Hills. From
Bagley's point of view, the best thing about the place was the
clear sign that Natives had used the place as an encampment.
With his duties completed, he set off in search of abandoned
artifacts. Others welcomed the unusually early marching
break in their own way. Some slept, while a few busied themselves collecting buffalo chips. A handful went hunting, and
the guide Morin shot an antelope, the first game, save ducks
and prairie chickens, that the force had enjoyed since Fort
Dufferin. The smell of roasting meat was powerful enough
to awaken Edward Maunsell from his slumber, which was
deeper than usual after gorging himself on the abundant supply of berries.

French called an early halt to the day's march to give
Macleod an opportunity to catch up. The journey to Frenchman's Creek was Macleod's third, adding some 300 miles to his
own march west. As his party returned to the force, his eyes
scanned the horizon, and he reflected on the extra distance,
which he couldn't help thinking was unnecessary. Poor command decisions during the preparation for the march resulted

in great hardships that could have been avoided. Wasn't it obvious to French that oats were more important than field guns? The men and animals need not have been so exhausted; the force could, no, *should* have been in much better shape.

Macleod considered himself partly responsible for the state of affairs. Certainly French had long ago proven unreceptive to advice, but the assistant commissioner knew he could have been more insistent. Still, Macleod also knew that to press for any changes was out of character. For the most part, he followed orders and did not question them.

But what he wouldn't have given for one man who actually knew the territory! Perhaps that had been their greatest mistake. Had they secured the services of a guide who was familiar with the route, how much easier would their march have been.

CHAPTER SEVEN

From the Cypress Hills to the South Saskatchewan River

Day 51, Cypress Hills
Rest Day

DAWN BROUGHT RAIN, and the coulee's natural depression acted as a great cup, collecting the falling water. Soon, the camp was uninhabitable. The commissioner had set out earlier in the morning in search of a more suitable location. He was frustrated because telltale white saline bands ringed most of the many bodies of water in the area, revealing all of them unfit to drink. Eventually, he found a nearby swamp that could serve the force's needs, and he gave the command to move out.

Once settled in the new site, the oxen needed to be reshod. The beasts were docile, and the only farrier (the others had deserted at Fort Dufferin) shod 20 by nightfall. A small party of men whose services were not required decided to explore. They climbed a close butte, and when they reached the summit, the men fell silent before the spectacular view. The rise was situated at the divide of the Cypress Hills and the western prairies. Towards the setting sun, the brown plains stretched as far as any could see. At their backs rose the bumpy green hills.

But what was truly magnificent were the huge herds of buffalo on the southwestern horizon!

Everyone knew that sooner or later they'd encounter the beasts, and they knew the herds would be large. But the knowledge hardly prepared them for the great brown mass that blanketed the distant plains. The men stood and stared until the sun slipped below the horizon. Finally, they hiked back to camp. As they walked, the distant dark sky suddenly exploded into streaks of red. The "bangs" of the explosions soon followed. The camp was sending up rockets, and the men hurried their pace, believing that they were assumed lost.

But it wasn't the absence of the explorers that motivated French to launch the rockets. They were sent up to signal Macleod, whose party had still not returned from the White Mud River. Macleod had planned to meet the force at Rivière au Courant, but the poor conditions there caused the force to move farther west. French wanted to be certain Macleod would find them. If they were within 30 miles, they'd see the exploding rockets. To be sure, French also dispatched a scout to return to the river and await the assistant commissioner. It was imperative that he arrive with the oats as soon as possible. Another horse had died during the day.

Day 54, Cypress Hills
Rest Day

The force stayed in camp on Sunday, August 30, maintaining the practice of worship and rest on the Lord's Day that French had established early in the march. On this occasion, remaining in camp also allowed Macleod's party to catch up.

Following the Sunday parade, French met with his officers.

"For those not keeping count, we've been on the trail more than 50 days," he informed them. "There have certainly been scattered problems with discipline, but few were unexpected or impossible to address. Under difficult conditions, for the most part, the men have done a good job. I'm issuing orders today informing them of the excellent service they've rendered since leaving Fort Dufferin. See that you inform your troops."

"Yes, sir," came the chorus of pleased replies.

"And officers, your service has been no less commendable."

"Thank you, sir."

"Sir," interrupted the commissioner's batman. "A couple Métis have returned to camp with buffalo! They're preparing to cook it right now!"

Finally, thought French, *the Métis are actually doing something of value.*

Edward Maunsell found a place near one of the fires above which roasted a great slab of buffalo. The aroma of cooking flesh tickled his nose, and saliva rolled across his tongue. He was hardly alone in his response. Every man gathered around the fires had a faraway glassy look in his eyes.

Unfortunately, the anticipation proved more rewarding than the realization. When Maunsell finally took a hunk of the meat on his plate, he found he couldn't cut it. So he took the steak in his hands and tried to rip off a piece of it with his teeth. Following an effort that would've shamed a hungry wolf, he met with success. But, chew as he might, he couldn't break through the meat.

"Mary, Mother of God! The meat is tougher than my saddle," he moaned.

"The buffalo on the edge of the herd are the old bulls," said one of the Métis scouts. "They live long, and their flesh is tough. It will be better when we pass closer to the herd."

"Live long! This one surely saw the arrival of Columbus!" exclaimed Carscadden.

"I sure as hell hope we'll meet some tender cows," added Maunsell. "In the meantime, toss me another piece. My boots are worn through; I can tie the meat on over the holes."

Day 55, 596 Miles West of Fort Dufferin
9 Miles Traveled

Macleod's party finally arrived with a large supply of oats, addressing the immediate problem of poor forage. Given their limited travel and free time over the past few days, French had tried to lift the men's spirits by promising them that a courier would soon be returning east. Most had put pen to paper in anticipation of sending word home. If French had read the letters, he might have given a second thought to sending them. Rare indeed was the missive that complimented his command. More common were criticisms, barbs born largely of hindsight. The men wrote of the scarcity of supplies, the inhumane treatment of the horses, the absence of appropriate organization and command disinterest in the troopers' welfare. The commissioner was oblivious to such complaints because he rarely communicated with the men and did not seek input from his officers. Perhaps it was a weakness in his command. But he could do little about most of the grievances, and to worry about them would only distract him.

Constable Chapman was dispatched to Fort Dufferin with letters and sensitive reports written by French.

Day 57, 627.25 Miles West of Fort Dufferin
15.25 Miles Traveled

Commissioner French was somewhat hesitant to order the camp to march on Wednesday, September 2. The previous day, the force stopped marching mid-afternoon when they stumbled upon a rare site with abundant grass, water and wood. French's estimated measurements plotted on Palliser's imperfect map suggested that they were not far from their destination, perhaps 100 miles from the Belly River, close enough to raise his spirits. But French suspected it would be the toughest 100 miles for the force. Food supplies were running precariously low, and the last 50 miles had seen hardly any good pasture. Scouts told him that the route ahead promised little more. French gazed off to the southwest and agreed that the situation was not likely to improve.

Movement on the horizon interrupted commissioner's thoughts. He rode past the front of the column and out to the advance guard.

"Constable, what do you make of that?" He asked.

"I've been watching it for a while, sir. Can't be sure, but I'm thinking it may be wild ponies," he replied.

The commissioner furled his eyebrows. "Ponies?"

"Too many of them to be antelope."

"But not too many to be buffalo," suggested French.

The words weren't out of his mouth when a pair of Métis burst from the ranks towards the animals, screaming as they rode. That proved it! French took the lancer's rifle and galloped off after the scouts.

Before he reached the Métis, French came within rifle range of a buffalo that had strayed from the herd. Silver Blaze hardly broke stride as French fired at the animal, taking it down in an instant. He continued on and joined the Métis, who had reached a narrow creek separating them from the bulk of the herd. He saw Lévéillé and Morriseau.

The trio quickly set upon the stragglers of the herd. Lévéillé fired; the ragged beast fell in its tracks. Morriseau was less fortunate. His bullet merely staggered the buffalo, which fell only after a second shot from French.

"Dress the meat," the commissioner ordered, "and take it to camp." French headed back to the column, relieved that scarcity of food was no longer a problem. As he returned, he saw others break free of the column to join the hunt.

Sergeant Major J.B. Mitchell had often heard the Métis spin dazzling stories about buffalo hunting, and he wasn't about to miss this opportunity. He and a companion moved ahead of the force and found a pair of buffalo grazing.

Henri Julien's drawing of the Mounties hunting buffalo, as it appeared in the *Canadian Illustrated News,* Fall 1874.

"Let's move in a little closer," suggested Mitchell. "You take the one on the left. I'll give the signal, and we'll fire together."

The men fired with a single crack. Mitchell's animal fell, but the other ran off. His companion followed in hot pursuit. Mitchell rode towards his prey, dismounted and stood above the animal. It was his first encounter with a buffalo, and he knelt for a closer examination. As he studied the beast, the one great eye that was visible cracked opened. With a raspy snort the animal suddenly reared up and lunged at him!

The buffalo's unexpected recovery threw Mitchell on his back. It also startled his horse, and the terrified animal bolted. Fortunately, Mitchell had held on to the lariat attached to the saddle horn, and his horse dragged him away from the buffalo's attack. Mitchell regained his footing, and to avoid the ongoing assault of the angry buffalo, he leaped and twirled, his red coat a swirling blur. As he danced, he used the rope to pull himself closer to his horse, until he was finally close enough to remount.

With a much larger target, the enraged and increasingly confident buffalo charged again. Mitchell drew his revolver and pointed it at the animal's forehead, unsure if a shot to its massive head would bring down the beast. The Adams smoked, and the buffalo fell like a huge boulder. Mitchell exhaled a ragged breath and slumped in his saddle. His arm hurt from the violent jerking of his horse, but he had a new respect for the animal that might have easily taken his life.

That night the men dined well on the buffalo French shot, which gave almost 1000 pounds of meat when dressed. French was angry that the Métis hadn't similarly dressed the other kills, but they assured him that there would be plenty more buffalo, making such hard work unnecessary.

Day 58, 644.75 Miles West of Fort Dufferin
17.5 Miles Traveled

Henri Julien was eager to kill a buffalo. The scene he witnessed the day before only heightened his desire. Was there another experience as western as hunting and killing a buffalo? It was a story he could tell wide-eyed easterners for years. With two companions and plenty of enthusiasm, he set out in the direction of the herd. The animals had moved on, so the trio scouted nearby gullies and bluffs for stragglers. As time passed, it seemed that the hunt would prove fruitless. Julien's comrades fell off, but he remained determined. The terrain changed dramatically, and the rolling prairie gave way to pockmarked ravines littered with sharp rocks and low brush. Julien soldiered on until he saw three buffalo nearby.

He rode quietly towards the three, but was still too far for a confident shot when the buffalo spotted him and bolted from their lair. Determined not to lose the opportunity, Julien fired at the slowest animal. The bullet struck true, causing the buffalo to shudder, but not to fall. Julien continued in hot pursuit and managed to sink another round into its flesh, again with little effect. Julien pushed Old Rooster harder, and a third shot finally brought success. The buffalo collapsed, gave a great heave and lay still.

Julien rode close and dismounted. As he surveyed his kill, the adrenaline seeped out of him, and he staggered with exhaustion from the intense pursuit. He looked down at his legs and discovered his pants shredded and bloodied. The jagged rocks and thorny bushes had taken their toll.

He heard a faint cheer, lifted his head and turned around. His companions stood atop a bluff offering their congratulations. Julien's eyes fell upon Old Rooster. Even on that hot day, steam billowed in great clouds above his body. But the source of the steam wasn't just sweat; the horse's flanks, legs and feet were bloody. The terrain alone hadn't caused the horse's injuries. Julien looked down at his spurs. They were bent out of shape. So intent on killing the buffalo, he had been oblivious of the horse and had spurred it unmercifully. It was a poor reward for an animal that had performed its duty so honorably. Overcome with guilt, the illustrator walked over to the poor animal, which nuzzled against its master's shoulder. Julien took note of the location of the kill so he could return with the Métis to dress it, and he led Old Rooster by the bridle back to the column.

French ordered the buffalo cut up and placed in a barrel of salted water. He was pleased that the salt they had carried for so long was finally being used.

Day 59, 644.75 Miles West of Fort Dufferin
20 Miles Traveled

As Lévéillé predicted, buffalo were abundant, and it was not difficult to kill more, so hunger was no longer a problem for the men. However, the force didn't lack obstacles on their march, and new problems quickly arose. The force crossed several coulees and camped in a deep ravine, which was a poor location, but the best that could be found on the day's route. Its steep slopes meant the men had to lock the wagon wheels while descending. Despite the precaution, more than one wagon overturned, and even careful drivers took nasty spills. Trees and other debris blocked the exit. French detailed 25 men to clear a path.

In hindsight, French had to admit that the coulee was the perfect place for an ambush.

Since the force's first encounter with the Sioux at Old Wives Creek, they frequently found abandoned Native camps and could sometimes see them traveling in the distance. French was worried about a hostile episode, but the troopers' growing familiarity with the Natives dulled their sense of caution, a fact noticed by a trailing party of Sioux.

Sioux pursuit skills were such that the troopers were oblivious to their presence. The braves watched the force with some confusion. They had heard rumors of the Red Coats' journey. Rumors from the east suggested that the newcomers wished to establish law and order, to offer protection to those who needed it. The Sioux had heard such stories before. The blue-coated Wasichus below the Medicine Line spoke similar words, but their smoking guns and grasping ways showed the truth of their intent. The words that prepared the way for the Red Coats rang hollow.

Even if their claims had merit, these newcomers hardly seemed capable of delivering on them, thought the handful of braves crouched atop the ravine watching the Mounties.

"Look at them. They are as children. They can't even help themselves. How can they help us?" one said with great derision.

"If they are even here to help us."

"If they are here to attack, we have no worry. They would not even be a match for our women."

"There would be little honor in taking their scalps."

"There is always honor in defending our way of life."

The others grunted their agreement.

"I trust no white man. I will not believe their words. The blood of too many brothers flows thick on the ground."

"Will we attack?"

"I will be ready."

Others joined the braves, but more remained concealed. They stood and loaded their guns. As they did, a shout came from below. A Red Coat pointed at them.

An observant sub-constable had seen the sun reflect off a rifle and spotted the handful of braves. He raised the alarm.

"Up there!" he cried, pointing to the edge of the ravine. "Indians! And they've got guns!"

Every trooper dropped what he was doing and rushed for his rifle.

The Sioux lowered their rifles; the advantage of surprise was gone and with it any desire to attack.

"Spotted Antelope, go and tell them we come in peace," directed the party's leader. "Ask them their intentions."

Spotted Antelope spoke French, and he showed neither hesitation nor fear as he nimbly slipped down the side of the ravine into the camp. On reaching the base of the slope, he met a Mountie who immediately escorted him to Commissioner French.

"Damn it! Where is Lévéillé?" shouted French. "We need him here to translate." The commissioner discovered that among the Métis' many annoying habits was their ability to be absent when most needed.

One of the sub-constables scampered off to find the interpreter as the Sioux stepped forward and addressed those present in French. The commissioner called to one of the nearby
men, who was fluent in the language.

"Sub-Constable, get over here. Listen to what he says and
translate it."

The brave spoke for a few minutes. Unlike the previous
encounter with Sioux orators, this one showed little in the way
of expression, adding only occasional hand signs for emphasis.
It was not the only thing that set him apart. He stood tall and
fit. His muscular body betrayed an absence of need and a presence of discipline.

If he is a representative of the Indians found in these parts,
thought French, *they will be a formidable presence indeed.*

Finally, the brave fell silent. "Well, what did he say, man?"
urged French.

"His French isn't quite intelligible sir—"

"We're not in grammar school, damn it! Give me the gist
of it!"

"Sir, he said that he has heard stories of the men in red coats
who come from the land of the rising sun. He has heard we are
good. He wants to hear it from our mouths. And, I think, he
wants more than words."

"Gifts?"

"Actions, I believe. I think he wants us to leave."

"Translate this: We come at the command of the Great
White Mother, who wants to ensure that all her red children on
the prairie are protected. We come in peace and will raise our
guns only to help her red children. If you obey her laws, there
is no reason to fear us. Tell him we are here to stay."

The sub-constable did as requested. As he spoke, the brave's
steely eyes took French's measure. When he finished, the Sioux
slowly lifted the barrel of his rifle. Most of the nearby men froze,
and a few fumbled for their revolvers. Only Sub-Inspector

McIllree had the presence of mind to train his rifle on the brave. But the Native continued to raise the point of his barrel until it pointed skyward. He fired it. Six more braves joined him with a speed that suggested some mystical ability.

The brave spoke again.

"He says that they fear no one and will take you at your word, for now. But they have been lied to before by white men."

Yes, it is true, I'm sure, reflected French. "McIllree, bring some gifts—tea, buffalo meat, ammunition and biscuits."

McIllree quickly returned with the goods and laid them before the Sioux. The braves began to talk. The onlookers assumed they were arguing about who should get what. The troopers would have been surprised to learn that they discussed whether they should take the goods, whether that was a sign of weakness. Finally deciding that the goods should be accepted as a sign of goodwill, the Sioux fell silent. They gathered the gifts, and the brave again spoke.

"We will go now, and tell others of your good heart. We will wait and see if your actions match your words."

With that they were gone.

"It's truly amazing what a few inexpensive gifts will do in the way of cultivating friendship with these people," said French. "McIllree, post a double guard tonight. The last thing we want is another surprise visit."

"Yes, sir."

Although he didn't say it, the commissioner was worried. He thought it unlikely that the handful of braves in camp represented their entire party. Their demeanor suggested that they were far too smart to allow all their braves to wander into a large camp, uncertain as they would be of the outcome.

"Is there no work to do?" barked the commissioner.

With less grace than the Sioux but with no less speed, the assembly dispersed. French turned and walked to his tent.

"You want me, boss?" asked Lévéillé.

French glanced back over his shoulder, sighed and kept walking. Lévéillé shrugged his shoulders and wandered back to the Métis camp.

Day 60, 682.25 Miles West of Fort Dufferin
17.5 Miles Traveled

It was Saturday, September 5, and Ed Maunsell was thirsty. Little water had passed his lips since Wednesday, and he longed to soothe his parched throat. So he was naturally excited when he saw what looked like a pond in the distance. As he rode closer, he noticed a dramatic increase in the number of buffalo tracks, until it was impossible to distinguish single indentations. For a moment Maunsell forgot about the water, as the tracks recalled recent heated discussions among the men. Most troopers were angry that French and the officers had hunted buffalo, while none of the men had yet been permitted to do so.

Maunsell forgot the griping, and his spirits soared when he caught the glint of the sun's rays reflecting off the pond. Clearly there was water here! But joy dissolved into disappointment when he was close enough to discover the would-be oasis was little more than a mud hole covered with a thin, stagnant layer of brackish liquid.

The order for a rest came. Maunsell got off his cart and wandered towards the pond's edge. He dipped his hand into the water and discovered that it was too shallow to allow him to even cup his hands. He pulled his hand out, and as the water ran through his fingers and rolled down his arm, his tongue was involuntarily drawn to his lips.

I've got to drink it, thought Maunsell. He looked around and saw many of his comrades staring at the pool, resignation written on their faces.

Maunsell retrieved a cup and a kettle from his kit, and returned to the pond. He took off his shirt, carefully scooped out the slimy liquid and strained it through the thin fabric into the waiting kettle. He dipped many times until he had a kettle full. He made a fire and brought the liquid to a boil. Then he added lots of tea, poured the mixture into his cup and slowly brought it to his lips. It was the most nauseating drink he had ever tasted, made all the more sickening with the knowledge that it was as much buffalo piss and chips as water.

Back on his cart, Maunsell tried to forget the experience, but it proved too much, and he wondered what else he might be reduced to doing on the march.

Day 61, South Saskatchewan River
9 Miles Traveled

Even though it was a Sunday, French marched the men because of the poor forage at camp on Saturday. He wasn't pleased when the Métis guide Morriseau showed him the site he had chosen for the day's camp.

"We can't camp here!" he shouted in an uncharacteristically heated tone. His temper had reached the boiling point, and he had long since abandoned any self-restraint in his dealings with the Métis.

"Tis a good coulee," defended Morriseau. "Give shelter."

"There's no goddamn grass! It's worse than yesterday!" bellowed French. "The horses need to eat. What the hell will we use as pasturage?"

The horses' condition was such that available forage determined the distances traveled on any given day. There hadn't been much since August, and even with numerous breaks, animals were dying daily.

"I guide the men. You feed the horses."

French had had enough. The Métis were without discipline, idle and totally undependable. He should have challenged Lieutenant-Governor Morris' recommendation from the start and damned the consequences. He would have to set the man straight. He stepped towards Morriseau until they were close enough to share the same air. He grabbed the man by the jacket.

"Listen, and listen carefully! Get out there and scout till you find us a place to camp with sufficient pasturage for the horses. Fail to find it, and don't return."

Morriseau raised his eyebrows, shrugged his shoulders, and replied with an unenthusiastic "*D'accord.*"

French strode away in disgust and ordered the march to halt. They would rest until the guide returned. He mounted Silver Blaze and rode away from the men, pulling up several hundred yards from the force, where he sat fuming. After some time, he composed himself and returned. While he waited for the guide to return, he reviewed his surveying figures and studied Palliser's map which, for all its flaws, had proven more reliable than the guides.

A few hours later, French's batman interrupted his musings. "Sir, Morriseau has returned."

"Over here, man." French waved the guide over . "What have you found? Good pasturage, I hope."

"Better! I have found the Belly River. A mile and a half away. We are at our journey's end! The Bow is just a mile south."

French sighed. "Is this a jest?"

"A jest?"

"A joke, man, a joke."

"No joke."

"We are at least 70 miles from the Bow River." French was confident enough in Palliser's map to be certain of that. "Take me to the river."

French and Morriseau rode to what the guide claimed was the Belly River.

It didn't take long to reach the river's edge, and when they did, French took out his log and tried to determine exactly where they were. The careful measurements he had taken since the force had marched north from the Boundary Commission Road proved their value.

"It's not the Belly. It's the South Saskatchewan."

Palliser's map suggested that the South Saskatchewan was at least another 8 to 10 miles away, but the inaccuracy of the distance was insignificant.

Morriseau responded with a shrug.

But pasturage was adequate, and with the fresh water, it would make an acceptable site at which to camp. French decided to move the men ahead. As they rode back to the force, however, French wondered whether Morriseau's poor guiding was the result of ignorance or deception. The thought that he might be a spy for the whiskey traders again crossed his mind. French concluded that the best course of action was caution. To that end, he decided to guide the force himself the next day.

Day 62, South Saskatchewan River
21.5 Miles Traveled

A small herd of about 50 buffalo ran close to the line of march; they never knew what hit them. The frustrated troopers didn't wait for permission to attack. The men at the front of the column broke rank first, and as those farther back along the line saw what was going on, the column eroded like a sand castle under the assault of a slow rolling wave. Riders forgot about the horses' condition and rode hard towards their prey. Drivers abandoned their wagons. The Métis guides had assured the men that there would be other, larger herds, but all were eager for that first kill, the one they'd never forget.

The Mounties' attack on the herd was a free for all, a chaotic mess. The men charged the buffalo and rode among them, kicking the dust of the dry plains into a cloudy veil. Shooters fired wildly, hoping they might hit the right target but unconcerned if they missed. Those who had exhausted their ammunition clubbed the animals with the butts of their rifles, more crazed than the beasts. Confused buffalo bellowed, and lusty men screamed. No one could be sure the massacre hadn't turned tragic. When the dust finally settled, 10 buffalo lay dead, and miraculously, not a single man was injured.

There were no complaints that night as the men gorged themselves on fresh meat. They had brought down some cows and calves, and the meat was a tender and succulent treat. The men would come to depend on buffalo meat for the rest of the march. It was a welcome addition and helped put some flesh back on their bones. And the animal that polluted the water was no longer quite so loathed.

Day 64, Dead Horse Camp (Great Sand Hills)
13 Miles Traveled

Joseph Carscadden pulled his blanket out of his kit and wrapped it around his shoulders. As of late, he was often cold. Ragged, threadbare clothing and worn boots slipped on over sockless feet would do that. The blanket was a poor shield against the cutting northwest wind that had begun its assault the night before. He could see the Great Sand Hills in the distance and cursed the commissioner for not taking the force closer so they might benefit from the shelter. Carscadden tried to forget his empty stomach. Plenty of buffalo was still available to eat if one wanted to be a savage and dine on it raw. The day before, great sheets of rain had fallen, and the buffalo chips that they used as a fuel for their fires were too wet to burn.

Over the past two days, six more horses had died. A handful of others could not continue on, and the commissioner ordered some sub-constables to remain with them until they were recovered sufficiently to travel. He had also taken other measures to aid the animals' plight. Today, he ordered each man to give one of his two blankets to a horse.

Evidence of the poor condition of the horses is shown in this Henri Julien drawing from the *Canadian Illustrated News,* Fall 1874.

Carscadden shivered beneath his remaining blanket pondering the same thing: the sorry plight of the force and the inept commissioner who caused it. A commander who had the best interests of his men at heart would quickly order a wagon broken up and its wood used for fuel. He had heard that French refused to do so because the wagons were government property! Imagine being concerned about that in the middle of bloody nowhere! And if the commissioner had any foresight, he would certainly realize that the two blankets needed for summer travel were sadly inadequate for the fall. Of course, had the commissioner any foresight at all, the force wouldn't be in this situation. He would have anticipated the need for food and oats to keep the horses strong. The men should have long ago reached their destination.

As he stared at the horses, their exposed ribs rippling the covering blankets, Carscadden could only shake his head in disbelief. The trooper who named this place Dead Horse Camp was right on the money.

French has gotten us into a situation, and he sees no way out, Carscadden reflected. *He's a poor leader. In fact, he fails to make the grade as a man. He's wanting in both feeling and honor. It's an extreme assessment but an accurate one.*

Carscadden went to his tent, put his head on his roll and drifted off to sleep.

Day 65, South Saskatchewan River
7 Miles Traveled

Commissioner French knew the horses were in desperate shape. The buffalo had eaten most of the prairie grass, so he had issued orders to double their dwindling rations of oats. But the previous night was the coldest yet, and two more horses had died. Morning brought no relief, as the temperature continued to plummet, and the bracing wind held a hint of snow. French was aware that even more dramatic changes in weather could occur. Last year around this time, a blizzard swept through the area east of the Cypress Hills. An early blizzard would have tragic consequences. If a few hours of cold killed a couple of horses, what would be the result of an extended cold snap? And if they lost the remaining pasturage beneath a blanket of snow....French was becoming increasingly alarmed for the force's safety, although he would admit it to no one but himself.

French called a halt to the day's march near a river that forked from the South Saskatchewan River. He thought it might be the junction of the Bow and Belly Rivers. If it was, then the force had reached the territory identified by Colonel Robertson-Ross as the location of the whiskey traders. Eager to discover if it was the sought-after junction, he sent two patrols to scout the rivers.

While French waited for their return, he was informed that a barrel on one of the carts had been broken open. It contained biscuits, and some were missing. Unknown to French, stealing biscuits had become a common practice among the hungry men, especially those who arrived in camp after the evening meal. Incensed, he ordered Macleod to bring before him the troopers on guard duty.

"Men, it has come to my attention that one of the supply barrels was opened without authorization, and biscuits were stolen from it. But I'm sure there are those among you who are aware of that," he added, carefully observing the men's eyes as he spoke. "I'm certain that the biscuits are long gone, but I'm confident that I can still determine the thieves. Please turn out the pockets of your greatcoats. He who stole them will undoubtedly have crumbs within."

The order shocked them because it was common practice for the men to carry biscuits in their pockets. They took them out along the way to nibble on. Everyone feared that crumbs would be found in their pockets and were silent as they followed his order. A shower of crumbs fell from the pockets of two men.

"Assistant Commissioner Macleod, will you please place these two men under arrest," directed French. "Ensure they are placed in irons."

The convicted men protested.

"I didn't do it sir! I don't know where the crumbs came from! I'm no thief!"

"Please, sir, they're old crumbs, pieces of rations I ate a long time ago."

"Sir, I have to agree with the men," interjected Macleod, who had been silent to this point.

"Pardon me, Assistant Commissioner!" bellowed French.

"It's not right to place these men in irons. Perhaps you are unaware, but the men do carry their rations in their pockets. It's reasonable to assume that they are telling the truth. Furthermore, our regulations do not give you the authority to make such an order."

French turned to the sergeants major who stood nearby. He was about to give them the order that Macleod refused to obey, but he could see in their eyes that they would not obey it.

French knew that Macleod enjoyed popularity among the men. He hadn't been concerned about it. Leaders lead and do not engage in popularity contests. But French also knew that this was a critical moment in the march. Earlier in the day a rebellion of sorts had occurred when B troop refused to break camp without breakfast. No food the previous day sharpened nerves. A dispute over leadership would throw the whole undertaking into chaos, and with the state of the men and animals and a possible turn in the weather, the result could be disastrous. He had to get the men into the whiskey-trading territory. By God, Queen and Country demanded it.

Still, for Macleod to challenge him here, in front of the men! It was as great a transgression of acceptable behavior as an officer could possibly make. He could see no way to address it in front of the men; to insist on the command might well incite mutiny. Mutiny! French capitulated. He'd deal with Macleod at his convenience. His shoulders sagged as he turned and strode back into his tent.

"Send for Sergeant Major Griesbach," he ordered his batman.

Moments later, the regimental sergeant major arrived.

"Griesbach, perhaps you are aware that the supplies were broken into and pilfered last night."

"Yes, sir." Although he didn't say it, Griesbach and every other man in camp knew of the theft and Macleod's triumphant confrontation with French.

"Inform the men on guard that night that they are to be fined $15 each for dereliction of duty." It was a steep fine, equivalent to 12 days' pay.

"Yes, sir."

French retired for the evening, still stewing over the encounter.

CHAPTER EIGHT

From the South Saskatchewan River to Fort Whoop-Up

Day 67, South Saskatchewan River
Rest Day
FEW FAILED TO NOTICE WHEN, more than two months into the march, French called a council of all commissioned officers. As the unusual command filtered through camp, the officers wondered why their presence was required.

"Gentlemen, let me cut to the chase. Based on my surveys, the Palliser map and the reports of two scouting parties, I can confidently say that we have arrived at the fork of the Bow and Belly Rivers. Colonel Robertson-Ross identified this as the location of the whiskey traders' forts, yet clearly there is little evidence to suggest their presence. All we have is this cask head, imprinted with the words 'Kelly, Bourbon,' found on the shore of the river." He held up the weather-beaten piece of wood.

"There is little indication that this site has had much in the way of human habitation recently, either. Scouting parties found three log huts, deteriorated and well on the way to full collapse. It's difficult to believe they are what has been called

Fort Whoop-Up. They're insubstantial and more likely to have been used by wolfers or hunters than traders."

"The scout Morriseau suggests Fort Whoop-Up is some 40 miles west of our present location. However, given earlier examples of his skill and knowledge, it would be irresponsible to heed his words," French scoffed.

Morriseau was, however, close to correct. Fort Whoop-Up was approximately 70 miles west; not only was the location identified by Robertson-Ross inaccurate, but what French believed was the Belly River was actually the South Saskatchewan River.

"It's curious that there is no fort, and I've sent Denny and Welch to scout and confirm that conclusion. Given that no apparent trails exist, I doubt they'll find anything. Still, the absence of whiskey traders confirms previous intelligence. Those who might have been here have likely retreated to Fort Benton to avoid the force," asserted French.

"It is necessary to consider our course of action," continued French. "As set out by our superiors in the Dominion government, the original plan was for the force to divide— half to winter in Fort Edmonton and half to return east with me. However, clearly our coming here has caused the whiskey traders and outlaws to flee. Therefore, it seems desirable to establish a permanent presence in the region under the command of Assistant Commissioner Macleod. But there seems to be no good reason to build a fort in this location. There is neither accessible grass nor wood and no indication that whiskey traders have even used the place. I am open to suggestions as to what we should do," he concluded, his final words characterized by a rigidity reflected in his stance.

For a moment, the officers were dumbfounded, uncertain they had properly heard their commander's appeal for advice. They quickly found their tongues, and took the rare opportunity to voice their opinions.

"I agree, there's damn little sense in staying here. The animals won't make it through the winter," asserted Walsh.

"And there's nothing to defend against," added McIllree. "That's truly baffling. I suppose they could have heard we were coming and—"

"We might question whether there will ever be anything to defend against," interjected French. "I understand that the trading firm of I.G. Baker serves these parts. Indeed, they own the alleged whiskey post of Whoop-Up. But they're honest businessmen who do not trade in alcohol."

"What about the reports of illegal trade and violence?"

"It seems more likely the work of isolated renegades out to make quick and easy money. Surely, they've heard of our approach and have returned to Fort Benton," emphasized French, who did not reveal Lawrence Herchmer as the source of his information.

"It seems that to move south makes the best sense. Puts us closer to the Fort Benton supply post. If we move north, we'll have access to Fort Edmonton, but as I understand it, it is also mostly dependent on Benton. Besides, most of A Troop is already there," said Macleod.

"From what the Métis told me about the Sweet Grass Hills, they seem an ideal location," suggested Mitchell. "Plenty of wood, good water and rich pasture. Right on the border, only about 100 miles from Fort Benton."

"Gives us easy access to communication lines with Ottawa. They'll probably want to stay informed about changing plans. Maybe even offer input," reflected Macleod. "And if we ensure a visible presence near the border, then I'd say those whiskey traders'll think twice about returning."

"It sounds like the consensus is to move south," said French. "We'll head southwest to the Sweet Grass Hills. If there is adequate water and pasturage and indications of illegal trade, we will establish a fort there, which will be manned by

Fort Benton, Montana, began as a fur-trading post of the American Fur Company in 1846. Located on the Upper Missouri River, it was ideally situated to dominate trade in the region. American Fur Company steamers plied the Missouri, arriving at the post with supplies and departing with great bales of fur, buffalo robes and wolf skins. In 1869, the U.S. government leased the fort as a military post, primarily to deal with the Blackfoot. With the stability provided by the army's presence, Fort Benton emerged as a service center for the many small communities scattered around it on both sides of the border. As a result, the popular cliché was that all trails ran out of Fort Benton, the "Chicago of the Plains." One of those trails was Whoop-Up Trail.

two troops. B Troop and the remainder of A Troop will move north to Fort Edmonton, and the rest of the force will return east with me as per our original orders." He paused.

"That's all men. You'll be informed of my decision." Before he could reach that decision, he wanted to hear the reports from Welch and Denny.

Day 68, South Saskatchewan River
2 Miles Traveled

The sun was still low in the eastern sky when Sub-Inspector Welch returned to camp. He made his way directly to the commissioner's tent.

"We traveled 30 miles west, sir. Not a sign of human habitation, neither shelter nor trail. All we saw were buffalo, thousands of them, moving south. They've pretty well decimated what pasturage there might have been."

"Good news. Not for the animals, but it allows us to continue south. Sub-Constable," French called his assistant.

"Sir?"

"Inform Inspector Walsh that I wish to see him."

"Yes, sir."

Soon, Walsh arrived at the tent.

"I've yet to hear from Denny, but the scouting reports confirm our suspicions that the territory is without a lawless presence. That allows us to carry through with our revised plans. Take the rest of A Troop and your own B Troop and move to the opposite bank of the South Saskatchewan River. Take the horses of B Troop as well. Remain stationed there until I send the order to move north to Fort Edmonton. You'll have it as soon as I receive Denny's report."

"Yes, sir."

"What are the numbers involved in the move?"

"There are 70 men and 57 horses."

"Very well. Move out before nightfall."

By the time night fell, Walsh and his men had forded the river. They remained there in limbo without the command to march north because Denny's party failed to return. The men began to sense the uncertainty of these command decisions and were beginning to despair.

Sub-Constable James Finlayson wrote in his diary, "We are lost on the prairie. No one knows where we are....Horses and oxen are dying fast. Provisions are getting scarce. Things look dark. Very cold."

Day 69, South Saskatchewan River
9 Miles Traveled

Much to the relief of Commissioner French, Sub-Inspector Denny's scouting party arrived in camp late in the afternoon of September 14. He confirmed that most of the territory he'd scouted was desolate and that he had sighted no traders, but Texas Jack still had quite a story to tell.

"We came upon a pair of Indians moving on foot," he explained to French. "We tried to catch up with them, but they disappeared into a gully. As we approached the gully, 50 armed braves emerged from it and stood side by side on the ravine's edge. Lévéillé tried to communicate with them, but they didn't understand Cree or French. Lévéillé figured that they were Sioux. I encouraged the Métis to approach the Indians, but when one of them waved a scalp and a knife, the Métis rode away."

"Uh-huh," nodded French, hardly surprised at the response of the Métis.

"My party would not return to the ravine. Instead, we decided to give it a wide berth. We rode north before turning west and followed the river back here. The Sioux trailed us the entire journey."

While French thought the Sioux behavior troubling, he was more concerned with Denny's description of the terrain on the route to Fort Edmonton.

"The tree line to the north was thick?" he asked.

"A wall of green, sir."

"Damn," muttered French. It would be impossible for Walsh maneuver the exhausted animals through such an obstacle.

"Good job, Sub-Inspector Denny. Dismissed." He called, "Sub-Constable, get in here."

"Sir."

"Write this message down and make sure it reaches Major Walsh without delay. 'Denny's report indicates that northern travel to Fort Edmonton is impossible given the condition of the animals. Follow the main body of the force to the Sweet Grass Hills. Collect any played-out animals that we may leave behind.' That's it."

The sub-constable darted from the tent and left French to contemplate the problem of the bony oxen, all close to starving. Unlike the horses, which could feed on the short pasturage left in the wake of the buffalo, the oxen could not eat the closely cropped grass. He resigned himself to the fact that there would be no relief until they arrived at the Sweet Grass Hills.

Day 74, West Butte, Sweet Grass Hills
Rest Day

On Saturday, September 19, Commissioner French grew increasingly concerned about the weather. Even the joy that greeted the first sight of the Rocky Mountains on Friday was tempered by the snow-capped peaks of the Sweet Grass Hills (Three Buttes). Winter would not be stayed.

The weather had grown colder in the past few days. Harsh winds blew in strong from the northeast, and with them came driving rain. At night, the men placed the wagons side by side and erected tents in their shelter to provide some small measure of protection. The animals were covered with blankets and tied up behind the tents, but three still died on the coldest night. In addition, they had abandoned more oxen to suffer the same fate as the 12 cattle that had died since they turned south from the South Saskatchewan River. The force's veterinary surgeon, John Poett, informed French that they'd died of simple starvation. Who would have guessed that the necessities of life would be so scarce on the prairies?

Even though the condition of the animals was bad, they were no longer French's primary concern. The men were exhausted, fatigue written on their faces and evident in their steps. He was no longer certain that they had either the physical ability or mental stamina to overcome sudden inclement weather. He heard the groans at the discovery of ice on a nearby pond. How would they react to a snowstorm? French spent many hours contemplating how the march had deteriorated to this low point. He found no answers, but then he wasn't given to questioning his own command.

To allow the men time to regain strength, French decided to remain camped near the Western Butte of the Sweet Grass Hills for a second day. His observations suggested the U.S. border was within 10 miles, but he felt it wise not to press the men. As far as locations went, this one had its merits. Pasturage and water were plentiful, and most importantly with the worsening weather, so was fuel. In addition to the trees, they discovered outcroppings of coal pure enough to burn bright.

To confirm his observations regarding their location, French ordered Macleod and a Métis to scout for the Boundary Commission Road, which he believed was nearby. They left in the morning but by nightfall had not returned.

Day 75, West Butte, Sweet Grass Hills
Rest Day

Major Walsh rejoined the force and reported six horses dead. Assistant Commissioner Macleod also returned from his unsuccessful scouting mission for the Boundary Commission Road. French was certain it was nearby, so later in the day, he ordered Macleod to search for it again. French took a separate party out to the south. Seven miles from camp they found a shack. It was on the Boundary Commission Road, long since abandoned and empty of supplies. But at least French finally knew their location.

Day 76, The Milk River
8 Miles Traveled

News of the force's proximity to the Boundary Commission Road and the international boundary generated excitement among the men, but that was dampened when the threatening snow became a reality. It fell hard, but thankfully with no wind. The rear guard, which plodded eight miles behind the advance guard, managed to stay on course by following the faint tracks in the snow. Without the tracks, the strange fog that further limited visibility could have spelled disaster.

Edward Maunsell was one of those in the rear of the column. He shivered as he watched his snow-covered comrades huddle in their carts, and the sickly, emaciated animals trudge through the deepening snow. He was exhausted when he arrived at camp hours later than the advance guard. The snow eased up, but he did not examine his surroundings other than to note the Milk River nearby.

When Maunsell awoke the next morning and stepped from his tent, he immediately forgot his sour mood of the day before. To the west, a great white blanket unfurled to the base of the Rocky Mountains, which commanded the horizon, and the sun sparkled off their snow-capped peaks. He climbed a rise, and to the east, an ocean of rolling brown extended as far as he could see. The snowfall had triggered the buffalo's southern migration, and thousands moved as one great body.

Best of all was the sight of the horses and oxen. The scouts had finally discovered a sheltered location with excellent pasture for the animals. The day was warming up nicely, and the snow would soon melt. The timing couldn't have been better. Had the animals been forced to endure the snow on the paltry rations that remained, Maunsell was convinced that the men would have been pulling the wagons themselves to their final destination.

As Maunsell looked around, he couldn't help but notice that not just the animals were in better spirits. While French might not have noticed it, the men were less on edge and no longer snapped at one another but chuckled as they went about their morning routine. Ever since the force had turned south a few days earlier, a new bounce could be seen in the steps of nearly all the men. The men needn't be expert scouts to realize that the change in direction meant that the force was approaching the end of its march. Of course, there may have been another reason for the enthusiasm that infused the men. The rumor was that Commissioner French would soon leave for Fort Benton, certainly cause for celebration.

The rumors were true. French, Macleod and Inspectors Jacob Carvell and William Winder were sitting in the commissioner's tent discussing operational matters that would mark the end of the march.

"As you know, the force will split up shortly. With the last eastern-bound mail packet, I sent a recommendation to Ottawa that the greater part of the force be stationed in this vicinity, near the international boundary and close to the whiskey posts, which are bound to be somewhere nearby. We'll then be able to keep them under constant surveillance. Its presence will act as a clear deterrent to whiskey traders otherwise intent on breaking our laws. I expect a telegram in Fort Benton granting approval," French informed his officers.

"Assistant Commissioner Macleod will oversee the construction of the fort and remain there once it is completed. He will command B, C and F Troops and the remainder of A Troop," explained French.

"Inspector Carvell will be in charge of D and E Troops. They will move to the Boundary Commission Road and will travel to Fort Ellice. I will join them at Wild Horse Lake, after I've been to Fort Benton. There, I'll communicate with Ottawa and investigate the alleged whiskey trade and last year's massacre."

French looked to Carvell. "We've got a long journey ahead of us through what may well be winter conditions, Carvell, so make sure you select the best of the remaining horses to take with you. I'll supplement them if I can with purchases in Fort Benton. Unnecessary equipment can be left in camp. Leave today and head south. Travel slowly and stop when you find good pasture. Take the younger Léveillé as a guide. He may be of value."

Carvell nodded.

"Macleod will join me when I leave for Fort Benton tomorrow. He will purchase supplies. Until he returns, Inspector Winder will be in charge of the troops camped here. And the camp should remain here until Macleod returns."

"Yes, sir," replied Winder.

Few men knew it, but French was making the plans to ensure that most of the men would never again see him. Fewer still would have been upset at that prospect.

Day 79, Fort Benton

Commissioner French departed for Fort Benton on Wednesday, September 23, accompanied by Assistant Commissioner Macleod, Sub-Inspector Brisebois, Assistant Surgeon Nevitt, two constables and several Métis, including Pierre Léveillé. They left the camp with little fanfare. French, however, left with the best wishes of the men that he never come back. Not a trooper among them didn't depend on tied-up rags to keep his hungry body warm, who didn't have gunny sacks wrapped around his feet to keep bare flesh from striking the ground and who didn't blame the commissioner for their desperate state of affairs.

With only four empty carts and the best remaining horses, French's party made good time, traveling the 100 or so miles to Fort Benton in less than three days. Their progress was hampered by a herd of buffalo estimated to be 70–80,000 strong. All agreed the spectacle was worth the delay.

Fort Benton came into view about noon on September 26. Its residents called it the "Chicago of the Plains." It might well have served as a supply center for the outlying regions, but otherwise little compared it to that Midwestern metropolis. In Macleod's eyes, it was a miserable place, filled mostly with incredibly popular grog shops.

As the party rode into town, word of the arrival of the northern lawmen spread. Curious onlookers soon spilled onto the main street, representing every social strata, from rich businessmen and their fashionable wives right down to the hard-living miners, wolfers, drifters and other ne'er-do-wells. Soldiers of the Seventh Infantry wandered out from their dilapidated garrison to size up the Red Coats. Prostitutes slipped out of their brothels, intent on sizing up other features, their eyes seeking big saddlebags that might indicate hidden bounty. Owners of the whiskey shops and gambling halls were also interested. The newcomers might not be soldiers, but they looked like them, and frontier experience had shown the locals that precious few of the military line didn't bend an arm or deal a card.

Ignoring the catcalls, suggestions and questions, the parties sought out the local telegraph office. French was keen on discovering whether his plans had been approved. When he found the office, he called back to the men to wait outside, and he noticed that the Métis were no longer there.

"Where in God's name are the guides?"

"Scouting out the local whiskey shops, sir," replied Macleod.

French shook his head, sighed and entered the office. He walked over to the clerk.

"I'm Commissioner George French of the North-West Mounted Police. I'm expecting a telegram from Ottawa, Canada. Has it arrived?"

"Yes, sir," replied the clerk. "It's been waiting here for you for some days."

French took the paper from the man and read it hurriedly. The Department of Justice had approved his plan to establish a fort near the Belly River rather than send troops to Fort Edmonton as originally planned. They also agreed that the commissioner and part of the force should return east.

What followed took the wind out of his sails. He would be returning to Fort Pelly rather than Fort Ellice, where the Department of Public Works had already begun construction of a barracks. French didn't know it, but Prime Minister Alexander Mackenzie's proposed transcontinental railway would follow the North Saskatchewan River, and Fort Pelly, on the Swan River, was much closer than Fort Ellice.

French had opposed Fort Ellice as the site of the force's headquarters because it was too far north. Fort Pelly was 90 miles farther north! He and his family would be isolated for months on end. It would not do. To add further insult, he wasn't even consulted on the matter! French wrote a hasty and perhaps ill-considered retort briefly outlining his objections. He'd be damned if he'd live in Fort Pelly.

"Send this immediately," he directed the clerk.

With that, he stormed out of the office, where some quick and fancy footwork only just saved him from bumping into a strikingly well-dressed man.

"Pardon me," growled French, repositioning his sword against his thigh.

"No mind," came the reply. "I understand that you're George French?"

"I am. And you, sir?"

"William Conrad, of I.G. Baker and Company."

"Conrad, very good!" French extended his hand in greeting. "I was going to look you up. Lawrence Herchmer of the Boundary Commission gave high praise to you and your firm."

"Very good. Haven't seen him in some time. He's well?"

"He's quite fine. Working some days east of here."

"I take it that you're in town for supplies?"

"Yes, among other things. And we're also in need of a good guide. One who knows these parts well."

"Charles, my brother, can assist you in finding a guide. His expertise is in distribution. As for supplies, if it's to be found in Benton, we'll have it. If it isn't, we'll be the first to get it."

"I do have a list. It's in with my papers, if you'll wait."

"I've a better suggestion. Why don't you and your officers come to my home for dinner tonight. After the meal, we can discuss what business there is."

"Capital idea."

"And have you made sleeping arrangements?"

"Not yet. Would you recommend an establishment?"

"Benton has come a long way in the past decade or so, and the rawness of life has given way to a certain civility. But, to be frank, sir, most of our hotels are characterized by their frontier heritage. I can't say that there's one I could recommend to a person of position. That's of no account, however. My home is open to you. You're welcome to sleep there."

"Quite good of you!" exclaimed French. "We'll be over later this evening."

By nightfall, they were seated at the dining-room table of William Conrad. French was about as surprised as he was pleased to find such class on display. It wasn't just the furniture and decorations, although the setting was impressive enough. Fine linen tablecloths, English bone china, sterling flatware, crystal glasses and high-backed oak chairs filled the dining room. The officers were in full dress, the men in tuxedos, and the women wore flowing gowns in modern eastern styles. The refined conversation touched on worldly subjects. Not a word was said about business.

After dining, the men retired to the study where the walls were adorned with oil paintings and lined with shelves of gilded books.

"Most impressive, William," commented French. He took a cigar from his host and settled into one of the leather smoking chairs. Also in the room were Charles Conrad, Macleod and Nevitt.

The men engaged in some further banter. Macleod's eyebrows raised when French entertained the group with stories of his early days in the army. He had not offered such tales on the march. Finally, they got down to business. The trader glanced over French's list.

"There's not a thing on here we don't have. As for the horses, you're quite fortunate. I recently purchased 15. Mustangs, but strong."

"What of a guide?" asked Macleod.

"I think I know just the man," answered Charles Conrad. "Jerry Potts."

"Yes." His brother nodded.

"Potts is a Half-breed. He's lived out here all his life. He knows the territory better than any man I could possibly recommend. Works for us now, but that won't be an obstacle. I'm sure we can work out suitable compensation."

"He'll be able to find Fort Whoop-Up?" asked French.

"It will be no more of a challenge than asking him to find the rising sun. It's not difficult to find in any case. It's right on the Benton–Edmonton Trail."

"We weren't aware of such a trail."

"A well-used route. Not sure why you'd be looking for Whoop-Up, though."

"Our mission is to stop the whiskey trade, and we've been led to believe that the fort is used for the illegal trade," replied French.

"An honorable mission." Charles shifted in his seat. "But even if men were there at one time, there aren't any there now."

"We heard there'd be upwards of 500."

The brothers laughed.

"Not likely."

"Are you suggesting there are no whiskey traders in these parts? How do the Indians get alcohol? And what of the massacre in the Cypress Hills last year? How can you be certain?"

"The fort's ours. We only use it for legitimate trade. Of course, there are always a few outlaws. We've probably traded with some of them. Can't control what they do once they leave Benton. But I can assure you that if we hear they are involved in illegal activities, we won't deal with them again. I think I can vouch for the other reputable merchants in town as well."

"And the outlaws involved in the Cypress Hills Massacre?"

"Can't help you there, I'm afraid. Likely long gone from these parts. Their kind doesn't stick in one place too long. But from what I heard, those boys were more interested in drinking whiskey than selling it."

The men made plans for the next day. French would go to the I.G. Baker warehouse and negotiate the purchases. Macleod would go in search of Jerry Potts.

When the business opened, French joined William Conrad, and they made their way to I.G. Baker's imposing white-fronted store near the banks of the Missouri River. The prices were good, extremely low, even for the horses, in the commissioner's opinion. He gave little thought as to why that might be the case, but I.G. Baker's proprietors were shrewd businessmen and not about to let their catch go before it was firmly on the hook. Before the morning was over, French had purchased enough supplies to outfit the force for the upcoming year. And by mid-afternoon the goods were already being loaded on a 16-oxen bull train.

Macleod began his morning by seeking out the sheriff. As he strolled down Main Street, he found the town already abuzz. The local grog houses had nothing as civilized as business hours, if the state of the folks stumbling in and out through their swinging doors was any indication. In a place like Benton someone was always ready to pony up 50 cents for a shot of whiskey. Macleod found the office and entered to discover a large man seated behind a desk.

"Can I help you?"

"Looking for the sheriff."

"You've found him. John J. Healy."

"James Macleod, Assistant Commissioner of the North-West Mounted Police."

"Heard for some time you boys were coming. Going to tame the wild northwest, is it?"

Healy had some firsthand knowledge of conditions north of the border, because he was one of the original investors in Fort Whoop-Up.

"How can I be of service?"

"Looking for some information on the men involved in the killings at Cypress Hills last year."

"Heard about that. Some kind of fight between traders and the Injuns."

"A fight maybe, but not in an honest man's book. Pretty much a massacre. Thirty Indians were killed."

Healy knew all the details about the Cypress Hills Massacre and could have drawn up a list of those involved. But he didn't want trouble for himself, which would certainly occur if word got out that he fingered the members of Evans' gang. Still, Healy knew the culprits were hard men, and it wouldn't hurt to get rid of them. Might actually make his job a little easier. It would certainly please the local businessmen.

"So you say. Can't rightly help you too much in the way of facts, but I imagine that if you head over to one of the whiskey joints, you might find someone who knows about it. When the boys are watered up, they're likely to reveal anything."

"Thanks," replied Macleod, and he left the office.

He could kill two birds with one stone. Charles Conrad was going to take him to one of the saloons to meet the scout he'd recommended. Macleod met up with Conrad mid-morning.

"Potts'll be 'round by now," Conrad assured him. "Don't let his looks fool you. He's a wisp of a man, but he knows more about the frontier than all the scouts in town. He can tell you if a buffalo was constipated from a week-old chip."

As Conrad had predicted, Potts was belly up to the bar. Macleod might have missed him if Conrad hadn't pointed him out. His shoulders were hunched over and his head hung low, so that in the soft light he looked like little more than a bump on the bar. He was dressed in well-worn buckskin from head to toe.

Macleod watched him for a while, but he saw little. Potts didn't speak to a soul, and the only movement was the occasional bob of his head when he threw it back to take a shot of booze.

"You're right. He's not much too look at," agreed Macleod. "Let's meet him."

The two walked over to the man.

"Jerry, how are you doing?"

Potts looked towards Conrad, nodded, but said nothing.

"This is James Macleod of the North-West Mounted Police."

Potts had seen the man's red jacket and knew before Conrad said anything that he was a lawman. He had heard from the Cree and the Blackfoot that they were coming, and he knew that the Blackfoot had been trailing the force for some time, biding their time while they determined the force's intentions. Perhaps this man Macleod would have been surprised to discover that the only reason his men were still alive was that the Blackfoot had promised Reverend McDougall to wait for the message they carried from the Great White Mother. Potts

Jerry Potts (1840–96), whose service as a scout and interpreter
with the NWMP was invaluable

꩜

knew all this, but kept his cards close to the vest. He'd get to
know a little more about these Red Coats before he confided
too much. When a man lives by his wits, he learns to keep
silent. Men who failed to learn that lesson were mostly dead.

"Macleod's looking for a scout to take him to Whoop-Up.
Told him you were the best around, and that you'd have no
trouble finding it."

"Yup." Potts knew where the force was camped, and that it wasn't more than 30 miles from Whoop-Up.

"You interested?"

"Yup."

"Great," said Macleod. "We'll be moving out tomorrow."

"I'll be coming, too," added Conrad.

"Do you know anything about the killing of those Assiniboines up near Cypress Hills last year?" asked Macleod.

Potts was silent for a moment. Those wolfers were a bad lot, and he despised the way they casually used poison. Although he wasn't afraid of them, or anyone else for that matter, he'd just as soon steer clear of them. But Potts was sharp enough to know that times were changing. Soon there'd be no place for wolfers and their kind. The northern lawmen might well be his meal ticket. He had a lot of wives and more children to feed.

"Mebbe."

Macleod waited for Potts to continue. His exasperation mounted with each passing moment.

"Well?"

"Look up John Evans. Buy him a round. The man has a mouth like a runaway mule. You'll know what you want soon enough. But don't wear your coat. And move your men west to the Whoop-Up Trail. It's well-wooded, with water and plenty of game," added Potts.

Macleod's eyes widened in surprise. Potts knew where the force was camped! His respect for the scout grew. Macleod and Conrad settled the details for Potts' payment and set a time for departure. When they left, Macleod followed Potts' advice. As he'd suggested, Evans was a braggart, and he told Macleod the details of the attack. When Macleod met with French later in the day, he was able to give a full report.

"Excellent work, Macleod!" he exclaimed. "I'll send the details to Ottawa."

French sent a telegram to Colonel Hugh Richardson, confident that they would be able to arrest those renegades involved in the bloody Cypress Hills Massacre. Because the culprits were on both sides of the border, he informed the colonel that they'd wait and make a simultaneous strike. All he needed was legal authority to arrest the Americans on their own soil. He was confident that the bureaucrats could work out the details. Eventually, they did, and the men were summarily arrested.

Commissioner French and Assistant Commissioner Macleod parted ways the next day. French was in a foul mood as he rode northeast to catch up Inspector Carvell. The Métis in his party were suffering the after-effects of too much booze and too little restraint. Macleod, Brisebois, Nevitt, Léveillé, Charles Conrad and Jerry Potts headed northwest for the Sweet Grass Hills. The bull train loaded with supplies pulled out not long after them. French and Macleod would never again meet as active members of the force.

Jerry Potts led Macleod's party as soon as they left Benton. Macleod had no reservations in giving him the lead since, from the start, the man demonstrated that he knew his business. He proved his value the first night out, when, after a short disappearance, he returned with a deer thrown over his horse.

"Chow."

The next night, he wandered through a river valley, returning with a handful of roots. He threw them into a pot along with some potatoes and the carcasses of a couple of rabbits that he'd brought down with disconcerting ease at 100 feet. The men claimed that even their mothers had never made such a tasty stew!

Macleod took a liking to the strange frontiersman. The feeling was mutual, and soon they rode side by side. Macleod learned that Potts had a Blood mother and a Scottish father and that his mother's people raised him as one of their own.

Modestly, he avoided any mention of the Natives' great respect for him. Macleod would learn about that soon enough.

Charles Conrad watched the pair with surprise and concern. He hadn't ever heard Potts string together more than a half-dozen words at once. He'd suggested the guide for that reason; he'd keep the secrets of the company. Yet, here he was in deep discussion with the Mountie. Conrad was unsure of the details of their talks. Potts knew all about I.G. Baker's business. Although they never admitted it, the trading company was one of Whoop-Up country's main whiskey suppliers. Fort Whoop-Up was actually one of their main distribution points. But the Conrads knew that the future rested in honest trade. Settlers were sure to follow the North-West Mounted Police and the rumored railroad would bring even more. Fort Benton was in an ideal position to supply the newcomers. But Potts could ruin everything. If he told Macleod of I.G. Baker's whiskey business, the North-West Mounted Police would look elsewhere for supplies and perhaps even ban the company from trading north of the border. Conrad feared the worst when he noticed Macleod looking at him with suspicion. But nothing was said.

Day 91, 869.5 Miles West of Fort Dufferin
10 Miles Traveled

After rejoining the force on October 4, Macleod waited two days before giving the order to march to Fort Whoop-Up. Potts assured the assistant commissioner that it was a three-day ride. As with most everything he said, his estimate proved correct.

Late in the afternoon, Texas Jack Denny gave a shout that brought the column to a halt. On the side of the trail lay a dead Native with so many arrows sticking out of him that he looked like a porcupine. Macleod rode back with Potts.

"What do you make of this?" asked Macleod, looking at the scalpless, dried out body.

"Assiniboine. Whiskey," replied Potts, his pointed words concisely underlining the tragedy of the North-West. Macleod was certain he could hear regret in the guide's response.

"Bury him," ordered Macleod.

Their Christian duty complete, the men continued on. As they rode, Macleod reflected on the odd twist in events that found him leading the force on its final leg of the journey. He still couldn't understand why the commissioner would abandon the march when the force was so close to achieving its objective. He knew that French wanted to return east to his family. Macleod was just as desperate to be reunited with his fiancée. And perhaps French and Conrad were right, and there would be no whiskey traders at Fort Whoop-Up. But after 800 miles, Macleod figured that French had earned the right to discover that firsthand.

Potts had been with the men for the better part of a week, and Macleod noticed that he hadn't said anything about the force itself. Of course, Macleod already knew him well enough not to expect an unsolicited comment. Still, he was curious about the man's opinion.

"Do you think we'll have much trouble at Whoop-Up?"

Potts considered his answer. He had never seen such a rundown, desperate bunch of soldiers in all his life. He didn't think they had much chance against a rowdy crowd, let alone armed outlaws. Still, if they all had Macleod's character, they might be able to hold their own. If they could, they'd be just what his people needed.

"Don't look too strong."

Macleod laughed. "Don't let appearances fool you!"

It was Potts' turn to laugh.

That night Potts led the men straight to a lush, green valley through which trickled a cool stream. With that kind of skill, he quickly became a favorite of the men.

Day 94, Fort Whoop-Up
10 Miles Traveled

On Friday, October 9, 1874, Fort Whoop-Up emerged on the horizon without warning. As the force rode closer, its structural details sharpened. It was a stockade, built of roughly hewn logs. The four-corner bastions were loop holed to allow rifles for defense. The weather-beaten barrels of brass cannon protruded from two loopholes. They could see the tops of various buildings inside the stockade, and a thin line of smoke crawled skyward. A flag, bearing some resemblance to the American Stars and Stripes, fluttered in the light breeze.

After traveling nearly 900 miles, the North-West Mounted Police had finally reached its destination. The march was over, and it was time for work.

PART III:
At Work in the West

CHAPTER NINE

The End of the Whiskey Trade

ON OCTOBER 9, 1874, the men of the North-West Mounted Police, sunburned and unimpressive in rags that fell from haggard bodies, stood on the sloping rise above Fort Whoop-Up. No one emerged from the structure to welcome them, but Assistant Commissioner Macleod would not take chances. The force had traveled halfway across the continent without a casualty, and he'd be damned if carelessness would cause one at journey's end.

"Inspector Winder, position the field guns."

The heavy guns had been a curse on the march, but when the men heard the order, they were suddenly grateful for Commissioner French's decision to bring them. As the Artillery Troop primed and readied the pair of nine-pounders, Macleod scanned the surrounding terrain with his field glasses. Some ponies grazed nearby, and a few dogs rested in the shade of the palisades. He called to Major Walsh.

"Major." He pointed towards the fort, "take some men and scout those ravines and gullies."

"Yes, sir," replied Walsh.

Fort Whoop-Up (ca. 1881), where the march west ended for the North-West Mounted Police

❧❦❧

Soon, Winder had the field pieces ready, but Macleod waited for Walsh to return before advancing. Upon receiving word that the trail leading to the fort was unguarded, he waved to Potts. The pair slipped down the slope to the fort. When they reached it, Macleod dismounted, walked to the gate and banged on it. After a few moments, it slowly creaked open. An old man appeared. A long, white beard flowed from his weathered face.

"I'm James Macleod, Assistant Commissioner of the North-West Mounted Police. We're now the law in these parts. Are there whiskey traders in here?"

The man's eyes grew wide, and the wrinkles on his face folded over as he listened.

"Nope. Ne'er no whiskey traders. And no traders t'all this time a year. All gone south. Just me and a few squaws tendin' the place."

"And who are you?"

"Dave Akers, at yer service."

"Can we come in?"

Akers then spied Charles Conrad. When he saw his boss nod slightly, relief flooded the old man's face.

"Sure."

Macleod called his men down and ordered a search of the fort. Except for the Native women who sat cloaked beneath their shawls, it was indeed empty.

"Y'know, we heard y'all was coming. Matter of fact, grub's on. Care for a mess a buff and beans?"

Macleod accepted the offer, and the men dined on roasted buffalo, beans and canned peaches as Macleod questioned Akers about the fort.

"So you say that this fort isn't used to trade whiskey?"

"Not one gallon has gone from this place to the Injuns," he replied. "Could a made a pile mind ya, a pile, but we ain't in that business."

"And what is your business?"

"Well, lee-gitimate trade, o'course," he squeaked. "Supplies for furs."

The story sounded a little too familiar to Macleod. He glanced at Potts, who gave a barely noticeable shrug. The assistant commissioner wasn't buying what Akers was selling, but his men could find no booze except a bottle that Akers claimed was for personal use. Without evidence that the place was used to trade liquor, he could do little.

"I hope your claims are truthful. But honest or not," declared Macleod, "any trade undertaken from this fort *will* be legitimate from this day on. And the Mounties will be staying around here to ensure it."

Macleod waited for a moment for his words to sink in.

"It's a bit late in the season to build a camp for the winter," he continued, "so I have a proposition, Mr. Akers. The Canadian government will buy this post for $10,000."

That was one way to ensure there'd no longer be illegal trade in Fort Whoop-Up.

Akers nearly choked on his buffalo. Once he finished coughing, he immediately looked at Conrad. Macleod caught the glance, and he too stared at Conrad. The shake of the businessman's head was slight, but perceptible.

"Nope," blurted Akers, his eyes watery and face red.

Macleod stood and walked to a corner of the room where both Akers and Conrad could see him.

"Let me be clear. The North-West Mounted Police force is the *law* here. If there is trade in alcohol, the traders will be arrested. And with a word from Ottawa, they'll be hanged."

When finished his short speech, he walked over to Potts.

"You know of a good location for a fort around here?"

"Yup. Just down by the Old Man's River. Close enough to keep an eye on this place."

With that, Macleod and the Mounties left Fort Whoop-Up. Three days later, Potts led them to the Old Man's River, where stands of cottonwood and broad meadows dominated the landscape. The area had fuel, building material, pasture and water. Macleod thought they could grow wheat on the surrounding land and grind it at the force's own gristmill. Best of all, the trail from Fort Benton was close and easily monitored. Macleod selected what he considered an ideal spot on a sheltered island in a looping bend of the river as the site for the fort.

With winter approaching, Macleod immediately set the men to building the fort. They staked out ground lines at 200-foot lengths and dug trenches to support the 12-foot cottonwood lengths that would serve as the fort's walls. The men were still busy cutting and stripping the cottonwoods when snow fell on October 19. A storm blew in a week later, and Macleod's concern for the horses heightened. In anticipation of a turn in the weather, he'd had the stables constructed first, but even with shelter, the horses were at risk because of poor feed. There was little hay to cut at this time of year, and it was difficult to find anyone willing to sell it at a reasonable price.

Hay was available at Fort Kipp, an abandoned whiskey post 18 miles down the Old Man's River, and Macleod sent a detachment under the command of Sub-Inspector Brisebois to collect it. He also considered sending some animals and the remainder of A Troop to Fort Edmonton, but conditions had not changed since September, when Commissioner French tried to send them north. Instead, Macleod decided to send the weakest animals—64 horses, 20 oxen and 10 young cattle—to Sun River, 200 miles to the south where good feed and water were readily available. Walsh was detailed to lead the 13-man party that included Potts. Macleod wasn't keen on sending Potts. He'd been active among the local Native bands, explaining the Red Coats' mission and offering assurances that they were there to help the Natives by stopping the whiskey trade. But Macleod wasn't sure the detachment would find Sun River without Potts' assistance. Constable Cochrane would remain at Sun River in charge of the animals.

Before Walsh's party moved out, troubling news arrived. Traders were peddling firewater not more than a few days' ride away. The information came by way of a Native named Three Bulls, who was camped on the trail outside the fort. Macleod directed Potts to meet secretly with Three Bulls and relay any relevant details to him. The assistant commissioner's caution was born of unfamiliarity with the men who had come to Fort Macleod since the beginning of its construction. Perhaps some were agents of the whiskey traders, and Macleod did not want to raise suspicion among them. Potts returned in the evening.

Superintendent L.N.F. Crozier (1846–1901) was charged with returning Sitting Bull and his followers to the U.S.

~◦❍◦~

"Three Bulls says a Black man operates a trading post at Pine Coulee, 'bout 40 miles from here. Name is Bond. He traded Three Bulls a few gallons of whiskey for two of his horses," explained Potts.

Macleod called for Inspector Leif Crozier and explained the situation to him.

"Crozier, I'm placing you in charge of arresting the traders. Select 10 of the best men and horses from the force and prepare to leave. Do not tell any of the men your destination. Potts will guide, so you'll have little difficulty finding Pine Coulee."

"Yes, sir."

The next afternoon Macleod gave Crozier a list of instructions. Liquor would be destroyed. Goods and chattel would be seized to pay the fines that might be imposed. Any robes and furs that Crozier suspected were the profits of illegal trade were also to be confiscated. Macleod thought that was a sound order because the sale of such goods was the only way to ensure that fines were paid.

Crozier and his detachment set out before dark and returned two days later with five men under arrest. He gave Macleod a full report.

"We found the traders about 45 miles from here. They did not resist arrest. They had two wagons, each containing cases of alcohol. Their other possessions included 16 horses, 5 Henry rifles, 5 revolvers and 116 buffalo robes. We confiscated all their goods. I might add, sir that our horses faired poorly. One broke down after only a few miles of travel."

"The animals may well hinder our ability to patrol," acknowledged Macleod. "I'll seek authorization to buy more. You've executed the mission in a most satisfactory manner, Crozier. Dismissed."

"Thank you, sir."

For the first time, Macleod exercised his authority as a judge, along with the force's inspectors, who sat with him to try the Bond party. The men were charged with possessing intoxicating liquors. Three men were fined $200 each, while the other two, who were hired men, were fined $50 each. The robes were seized and the men placed under guard. The next day a man named Waxy Weatherwax arrived from Fort Benton to pay the fines of all the men except William Bond's, the guide and interpreter of the men who traded the liquor to Three Bulls. Macleod planned to sell the man's belongings, but because the sale wouldn't realize the amount of the fine, he also ordered that Bond remain imprisoned. But in early December, Bond escaped, and an angry Macleod demoted the Mounties involved.

The arrest of the Bond party was timely, if only because the troopers were in need of warm clothing. Macleod supplemented buffalo robes he had purchased in Fort Benton with the 50 seized from the whiskey traders. The men were in good spirits when they learned that they'd no longer have to depend on layered rags for warmth. Macleod also had caps and mitts made from seized robes unfit for other use. And the men's ability to withstand the falling temperatures was also aided by the welcome new regimen of regular meals that were not the wet and dry of the march. Buffalo were within hunting range, and I.G. Baker bull trains had already delivered the supplies ordered at Fort Benton. The men were appalled at the high prices: $1 for a can of fruit! Nevertheless, sales were brisk and purchases were made on credit because the Mounties were yet to be paid. Despite the clothes and the food, the long march had taken its toll on the men, and many fell sick. One day in November, 45 men were laid low with colds.

When the bull trains arrived, I.G. Baker employees began to build a trading post near the fort. The Conrad brothers also built a house, where Macleod lived during construction of the fort. Soon, other trading companies from Fort Benton joined I.G. Baker. The men were especially pleased when a billiard room was built. It wasn't long before a small village sprang up around the fort, which French had ordered be called Fort Macleod before he returned east. Both men and officers were pleased with the name. By early December, the fort was nearly complete. The stables and men's quarters were usable, and most of the officers bunked in the kitchen while their quarters, the last constructed as per British military tradition, were built.

When Jerry Potts led the NWMP to the Old Man's River and the site he recommended as appropriate for Fort Macleod, the Mounties were pleased with his choice. However, many were less interested in the abundance of available resources than they were with a local Métis family, which included several eligible daughters. With high pickets around it, the fort enclosed an area of approximately 200 feet by 200 feet and a variety of buildings, including living quarters, messes, stables and a hospital, all of which faced a large square. While flooding was a concern, Macleod reported to Commissioner French in October 1874 that "there are no indications that [the river] ever rises so high as the site of the fort." Flooding eventually did necessitate the relocation of the fort a decade later. Fort Macleod was the force's headquarters from 1876 to 1878.

While Macleod was pleased with the rapid construction of
the fort, his greatest pleasure came from the effect of the Mounties' presence on illegal whiskey operations. In addition to the
arrest of the Bond party, the men had found at least one liquor
cache. On December 4, 1874, Macleod wrote to Commissioner
French, outlining the force's admirable progress:

> I am happy to be able to report the complete stoppage of
> the whiskey trade throughout the whole section of this country,
> and that the drunken riots, which in former years were almost
> of a daily occurrence, are now entirely at an end; in fact, a more
> peaceable community than this, with very large numbers of
> Indians camped along the river, could not be found anywhere.
> Everyone [is] united in saying how wonderful the change is.
> People never lock their doors at night, and have no fear of
> anything being stolen, which is left lying about outside;
> whereas, just before our arrival, gates and doors were all fas-
> tened at night, and nothing could be left out of sight. So
> strong was the Indian's passion for whiskey, they could not be
> kept out of traders' houses by locks and bars; they have been
> known to climb up on the roofs, and endeavor to make their
> way through the earth with which the houses are covered, and
> in some instances they slid down through the chimneys.

French was somewhat less confident, and perhaps more real-
istic, about the force's effect on the whiskey trade, as he revealed
in his yearly report to the Minister of Justice in January 1875.

> I have no doubt that a certain amount of liquor traffic will be
> carried on in the vicinity of the Boundary Line, and I feel certain
> that a good deal will be done in the Cypress Hills during the
> present winter, but I would hope that during the present year
> we will be able to make such dispositions as will completely erad-
> icate the trade from the Cypress Hills to the Rocky Mountains.

The arrival of the North-West Mounted Police essentially put an end to the whiskey trade. Key suppliers in Fort Benton, including nearly all of the important trading companies located there, realized that money could be made supplying the settlers who would inevitably arrive. They could see no reason to continue to trade booze. Nevertheless, independent operators persisted in the illicit trade, and over the next year or so, the Mounties occasionally arrested such individuals.

Throughout 1875, the North-West Mounted Police spread out across the West. Another detachment was located at Fort Kipp, and by the close of the year, two additional forts were established: Fort Walsh, near the site of the Cypress Hills Massacre, and Fort Calgary at the junction of the Elbow and Bow Rivers. The incidence of illegal whiskey trading decreased dramatically. The presence of the North-West Mounted Police had removed the scourge of the West.

CHAPTER TEN

Earning Native Trust

ON MAPS, THE MOUNTIES' 900-MILE MARCH took them deep into the Dominion of Canada's North-West Territories. In reality, the completion of the march found the force in the heart of Blackfoot territory, which stretched from the Red Deer River south to the Missouri River. The Mounties knew little about these Natives who, unlike most other Plains tribes, had thus far resisted white intrusion into their territory. But stories told by trappers, traders and missionaries suggested that the Blackfoot were a fierce people, determined to protect their way of life and their land. Lieutenant-Governor Alexander Morris believed the rumors. He described the Blackfoot as "some of the most warlike and intelligent but intractable bands of the North-West."

As Fort Macleod neared completion, and the whiskey trade was brought under control, Macleod turned his attention to the imposing Blackfoot. Earning their trust and confidence had been a primary reason for the creation of the North-West Mounted Police. If the Natives were not convinced that the Red Coats acted in their best interests, they would likely resist a white presence in their territory. As the Mounties were charged with preparing the way for settlement, a failure to prove their goodwill to the Blackfoot would be disastrous. Macleod was aware of the weighty responsibility, and in November 1874, he directed Jerry Potts to visit the local Blackfoot bands to explain the force's peaceful mission and to invite them to Fort Macleod. Potts understood the Blackfoot well enough to know that his mission would be difficult.

The Blackfoot consisted of three bands—Blood, Peigan and Blackfoot—that shared the Blackfoot language.* At times the bands allied with neighboring Sarcee and Gros Ventre, creating a powerful and feared alliance known as the Blackfoot Confederacy. They warred with the Cree, Crow, Assiniboine and occasionally the Sioux to protect the rich hunting grounds in their territory. They also raided enemy tribes to demonstrate bravery, steal horses or avenge past raids. And they excelled at it. By the 19th century the Blackfoot had established themselves as one of the great Plains peoples.

But even the powerful Blackfoot could not defeat the white man's firewater. The whiskey traders crossed the Medicine Line about 1870, when merchants out of Montana built what would come to be known as Fort Whoop-Up at the fork of the Old Man's and St. Mary's Rivers in Blood territory. Initially, they stocked the fort with all sorts of trade goods, but soon found whiskey and rifles to be the most popular items. When other Montana merchants saw the money that could be made in the booze business, numerous trading posts quickly sprang up in what rapidly became known as Whoop-Up country.

---

*For clarity, the Blackfoot band is referred to as Siksika, the Blackfoot word for their band, while Blackfoot will indicate the grouping of all three bands. Also, an alternative spelling for Peigan is Piegan.

The sudden availability of liquor had a devastating impact on the Blackfoot. Liquor was foreign to their way of life, and they had a difficult time adjusting to it. The greatest problem was the violence that accompanied the drinking. They turned on the traders and fellow band members. Others met with less violent but equally tragic ends: some froze to death while drunk; some starved. Unscrupulous traders ensured the Natives wasted their trade goods on whiskey. Many more died at the hands of the firewater itself, since it was often fortified with everything from iodine and turpentine to gunpowder. The effects of liquor decimated communities. Of those who didn't die, many were left destitute and demoralized.

The missionary Father Constantine Scollen, long familiar with the Blackfoot, visited them in the summer of 1874 and reported on the changes that had occurred: "It was painful for me to see the state of poverty to which they had been reduced. Formerly they had been the most opulent Indians in the country, and now they were clothed in rags, without horses and without guns." The situation even affected the balance of power with the Cree, who were too far north to trade often at the southern forts, and had fewer problems with liquor. They found it increasingly easy to take control of Blackfoot territory.

The Blackfoot knew the white man's firewater was destroying them, but even the respected chiefs, who advised them to avoid the harmful trading posts of Whoop-Up country, failed to be persuasive. So, when Reverend McDougall brought word of the impending arrival of the North-West Mounted Police and promised that the Red Coats would remove the whiskey traders, many Blackfoot cautiously welcomed the news. One who did was the powerful chief Crowfoot.

Crowfoot was born a Blood but raised as a Siksika like his father. As a young man, he demonstrated great bravery against the enemy, and his reputation attracted many warriors who

The NWMP earned the respect of Blackfoot chief Crowfoot (1830–90), which helped to convince him to make treaty.

wished to raid with him. Before the age of 30, he had been wounded six times, each injury a mark of his courage. By that age, he also had three wives and a large herd of horses, both indications of his wealth and hunting prowess. In the mid-1860s, when the chief of Crowfoot's band died, many rejected tradition and chose to follow him rather than the old chief's son. In 1865, Crowfoot became chief of the Big Pipes Siksika band. Throughout the late 1860s, his wisdom and bravery continued to impress the Siksika, and upon the death of the Siksika head chief in 1872, Crowfoot was chosen to replace him. By the summer of 1874, he was one of the most powerful Blackfoot chiefs.

Crowfoot was pragmatic. When he learned that the Red Coats had come to help his people, he was not concerned that they were white. As a chief, Crowfoot's concern was the welfare of his people, and he did not worry about the skin color of those who might help them. With resignation and some hope, the chief said as much to the Reverend McDougall upon hearing that the Red Coats would stamp out the illegal whiskey trade and bring law to the country:

> *My brother, your words make me glad. I listened to them with not only my ears, but with my heart also. In the coming of the Americans, with their firewater and quick-shooting guns, we are weak, and our people have been woefully slain and impoverished. You say this will be stopped. We want peace. What you tell us about this strong power which will govern with good law and treat the Indian the same as the white man makes us glad to hear. My brother, I believe you, and am thankful.*

Despite his words, Crowfoot harbored some doubt. The American traders had said they brought their trade goods to help the Blackfoot. Crowfoot had believed them and had initially supported trade with them. But the Americans had lied. They proved themselves harmful to the Blackfoot, and Crowfoot eventually advised avoiding them, but it had not been easy to persuade those who had come to need the firewater's burn. Crowfoot wondered whether the Red Coats also lied. He would not be deceived again. To discover whether their actions would match McDougall's assurances, Crowfoot sent Three Bulls to Fort Macleod with the information about the whiskey traders. He was pleased when the Red Coats captured them. On December 1, Crowfoot joined other chiefs and head-men in a visit to Fort Macleod.

The Siksika chief approached the fort warily, even after receiving assurances that he would be safe there. He arrived dressed little differently than a brave but carried with him an eagle wing, symbolic of his position as an important chief. Macleod welcomed him, and Crowfoot was happy to meet the man his people called Stamix Otokan, or Bull's Head, because of the buffalo head mounted above the entrance to his head-quarters. Macleod was prepared to outline the Mounties' mission to Crowfoot, but the chief wanted to hear the Red Coat chief's words spoken at council, where a man's words were not taken lightly. Potts had informed Macleod of Crowfoot's importance, and Macleod readily agreed to the request. Crow-foot and other chiefs joined Macleod and his officers at council in early December.

Macleod spoke first. "I'm James Macleod, Assistant Com-missioner of the North-West Mounted Police, representative of the Great White Mother in these parts," he said through Potts. "I've asked you here to explain our mission. I want no misunderstanding about the laws of the Great White Mother, which we have come to enforce.

"The Great White Mother has laws that must be obeyed by whites and Indians alike. There's to be no killing and no steal-ing. And that includes horses. Women and children are not to be harmed. If the laws are broken, the culprit," Macleod paused briefly for emphasis, "and let me again say that it makes no dif-ference if he his Indian or white, will be punished. No one will be punished for something that he did not know was wrong. Obey the laws of the Mounties. They are for your protection.

"Some of you might be afraid that we have come to take your land. That is not our objective," assured Macleod. "We sim-ply want to ensure that all who live here can do so in peace."

Macleod's words appealed to Crowfoot. He rose and shook hands with Macleod and the other officers in the room. Then he bared his arm, a sign of his own peaceful intent, and responded to Macleod's speech.

"I look to the Sun," began Crowfoot, as he lifted his hand skyward, "and thank it for telling the Great White Mother to send these Red Coats. I thank the Red Coats for coming. Their words are what we want to hear. Their actions are what we want to see. The traders' liquor has been more devastating than enemy rifles. The Red Coats can save us from them. Then we may have peace. That is what my heart also desires.

"You are a brave man, Stamix Otokan," added Crowfoot. "The law of the Great White Mother must be good when she has a son like you. We will obey the law."

The council ended with both parties on good terms. Crowfoot believed that in Macleod he had found a man of his own heart, and it was the beginning of a long friendship. The Siksika chief immediately began enforcing the rules of the Red Coats by forbidding his young warriors to raid enemy tribes.

Generally, Crowfoot's authority prevailed, especially because alcohol was no longer available to fuel Siksika aggression. Occasionally, because of the rashness of youth, warriors raided anyway. When he discovered the news, Crowfoot had the stolen horses returned to their rightful owners, a course of action that could not have been imagined a year before. To appease the braves, Crowfoot replaced the horses he had taken with those from his own herd.

The condition of the Blackfoot reversed quickly and dramatically. On a visit to the bands in the summer of 1876, Father Scollen reported that since the arrival of the North-West Mounted Police "the Blackfoot are becoming more and more prosperous. They are now well clothed and well furnished with horses and guns. During the last two years, I have calculated that they bought 2000 horses to replace those they had

given for whiskey. They are forced to acknowledge," Scollen
added, "that the arrival of the Red Coats has been to them the
greatest boon."

Crowfoot would not have disagreed. In the summer of
1875, he met with Reverend McDougall and admitted as
much. He declared to the reverend the Red Coats were honest
men, whose just ways had ensured that the violence of the
Whoop-Up days was a fading memory. But Crowfoot was troubled by a new problem—peace made the prairies more attractive for settlement. Métis and white settlers were moving onto
territory that had traditionally been Blackfoot In the mid-
1870s, their numbers weren't great, but Crowfoot and other
Blackfoot leaders were concerned. Already the buffalo herds
were noticeably smaller, and the hunts not as plentiful as in
previous years. If settlers chose to move into Blackfoot hunting territory, they would be a further disruption. Without the
buffalo, it would be impossible to maintain the Blackfoot way
of life. Crowfoot had asked McDougall what might be done
to address the problem.

"Your situation is not unlike that of the Indians in the eastern parts of Canada. Treaties were signed that set land aside
for them and ensured that their rights would be respected,"
explained McDougall. "It will be the case here. In due time
treaties will be made, and a settled condition created in this
country wherein justice will be given to all."

A few weeks later, a representative of the Dominion government confirmed McDougall's comments. Near Blackfoot
Crossing, Crowfoot met the commander of the Canadian Militia, Major General E. Selby-Smyth, who had been assigned by
Prime Minister Alexander Mackenzie to report on the effec-
tiveness and general efficiency of the North-West Mounted
Police. Macleod and a small detachment escorted Selby-Smith
for much of the western journey, and the assistant commissioner was present during the council with Crowfoot.

In his report, Selby-Smyth described the encounter:

> *Round a large council fire on the high cliffs...these chiefs received myself and my staff after night fall, and with the solemn dignity of their race, they each in turn delivered a speech, the sum of which was in effect the great satisfaction they derive from the presence of the Mounted Police in their country, the security and peace that had succeeded the anarchy, disorder and drunkenness, the prosperity which had replaced poverty and want—that whereas in former times their young men were the victims of unscrupulous traders who had bartered ardent spirits for their horses and buffalo robes, by which they were reduced to squalor, misery and crime—now that the infamous liquor trade had been completely put an end to by the presence and activity of the police, all was changed for prosperity and contentment as well as security for life and property, horse-stealing had become rare, because now the young men could procure what horses they required in exchange for buffalo robes, they could lie down in their lodges at night feeling security from depredation.*
>
> *It may not be out of place to mention here that by the American officers in their North-West outpost as well as by the white inhabitants, half breeds and Indians, with whom I came into contact, Lieutenant-Colonel Macleod is held in very high esteem: he has gained the respect, esteem and confidence of all classes—and the intimate acquaintance, formed in company with him of over 700 miles of my journey has similarly impressed me in his favor, as an officer eminently adapted for the post he occupies.*

Crowfoot raised the most important matter of the council: "What will the Great White Mother do to help my people?"

"My government's objective is to deal fairly with all tribes in Her Majesty's domain and to extend uniform justice to the Indians of the Plains," replied Selby-Smyth.

Crowfoot found some comfort in such words. Certainly the efforts of the Red Coats suggested that these newcomers meant what they said. But Assistant Commissioner Macleod said that the Blackfoot could keep their land, and the arrival of settlers seemed to cast that pledge in doubt. In the interests of his people, Crowfoot needed more than the assurances of Macleod, McDougall and Selby-Smyth. He wanted the Great White Mother to identify exactly what she would do to help the Blackfoot. In the fall of 1875, Crowfoot called for a council of the Blackfoot to discuss the issue. Debate was heated, but consensus soon emerged. The Natives had a local Frenchman draft and translate their concerns.

The petition first outlined Blackfoot complaints.

...*white men have already taken the best locations and built houses in any place they pleased in your petitioners' hunting grounds; that the Half-breeds and Cree Indians hunt buffalo, summer and winter, in the center of the hunting grounds of the Blackfoot nation since four years* [ago]; *that American traders and others are forming large settlements on the Belly River, the best winter hunting grounds of your petitioners; that no Indian Commissioner has been seen by us.*

The petitioners ask that an Indian Commissioner visit us at the Hand Hills and [state] *the time of his arrival there, so that we could meet with him and hold a Council for putting a* [stop] *to the invasion of our Country, till our Treaty be made with the Government. The petitioners are perfectly willing* [that] *the Mounted Police and the Missionaries remain in our country, for we are indebted to them for important services. The petitioners ask for the removal of American traders and that a Hudson's Bay Company build a post to replace them. Your petitioners feel perfectly confident the representative of our Great Mother, Her Majesty the Queen, will do justice to her Indian children.*

The petition was forwarded to Lieutenant-Governor Alexander Morris, who took it to mean that the Blackfoot wanted to make treaty. The Blackfoot, however, wanted protection with no loss of territorial control. Crowfoot likely supported the idea of a treaty that offered protection. The assistance of the Red Coats and his personal friendship with Macleod undoubtedly influenced his perspective.

But Crowfoot would soon no longer be able to depend on Stamix Otakan. Macleod was preparing to resign as assistant commissioner in late 1875. On November 15, he was appointed the stipendiary magistrate for the western part of the North-West Territories, a position created by the North-West Territories Act in April, which would come into effect on January 1, 1876. In order to take up his new position, Macleod was required to surrender his commission with the police. With regret, the men of the force said goodbye to one of their most popular officers. Crowfoot shared in their regret.

CHAPTER ELEVEN

The Feathers of the Bird

JAMES MACLEOD'S DEPARTURE from the force was short-lived. In the summer of 1876, the Committee of the Privy Council recommended that Commissioner French be informed that his services were no longer required. In support of its position, the committee noted that "the condition of the force and particularly of those two divisions more immediately under the command of Colonel French is very unsatisfactory...." French unsuccessfully tried to defend himself against the accusations, but was allowed to resign to avoid the embarrassment of being fired. On July 20, 1876, Macleod was appointed Commissioner of the North-West Mounted Police. He also retained his position as magistrate.

One of his first responsibilities was to lead an escort accompanying David Laird, the newly appointed lieutenant-governor of the North-West Territories, to Forts Carlton and Pitt where Treaty 6 would be signed with the Cree. When the Blackfoot learned of the council with the Cree, they were even more insistent that a representative of the Great White Mother meet with them to discuss protection of their interests. The government was eager to meet their demands, but before a council could be held, an incident along the international border required the immediate attention of the North-West Mounted Police.

During the summer of 1876, the American army suffered shocking setbacks to the Sioux and their Native allies. The Sioux were in many respects similar to the Blackfoot—respected, feared and resistant to white expansion into their territory. They had been fighting the Americans since the 1860s and had enjoyed considerable success in protecting their homelands. But in July 1876, the Sioux won two decisive and unexpected victories that dwarfed previous accomplishments. Americans were staggered to learn of General George Crook's defeat at the Battle of the Rosebud and the decimation of General George Custer's command at the Battle of the Little Bighorn.

The losses energized the American army, and as summer gave way to fall, soldiers intent on revenge doggedly pursued the Sioux. Many Sioux followed Sitting Bull, a war chief and holy man who had a considerable reputation among both Natives and whites. He struggled to find a course of action that would avoid surrender and defeat. In desperation, Sitting Bull led his people across the Medicine Line into Canada, where he hoped to be given a reservation, as had Santee Sioux refugees in the 1860s.

The American government informed the Dominion government of the situation, who told Macleod that the Sioux might come to Canada and use it as a safe haven from which to attack the Americans. The commissioner increased the detachments stationed at Fort Macleod and Fort Walsh in anticipation of their arrival. But before the Sioux arrived, Sub-Inspector Cecil Denny delivered a troubling report to newly appointed Assistant Commissioner A.G. Irvine, giving him even greater cause for concern.

In early July, Denny had traveled to a Blackfoot camp to arrest a prisoner. Crowfoot was there.

Fort Walsh in the late 1870s. Built in 1875 and named after James M. Walsh, it became western headquarters of the NWMP in 1878.

Denny told Irvine, "Crowfoot talked about a twist of tobacco that he said came from the Sioux accompanied by a message. The Sioux wanted the Blackfoot to join them in a war against enemy tribes and the Americans. In return for their support, the Sioux promised the Blackfoot horses and women that they had taken from the Americans. They also told the Blackfoot that, after they killed all the whites, they would come and help the Blackfoot exterminate the whites on this side of the border."

The story drew Irvine's full attention.

"They said that the Sioux knew the soldiers on this side were weak, and it would take but a short time to capture any forts they had built here, as they had taken many strong stone forts from the Americans with small loss to themselves."

"Lord," uttered Irvine. "How did the Blackfoot reply?"

"They said that they would not join the Sioux on such terms. They would not help them fight the whites because the Red Coats were their friends. They sent the tobacco back."

Irvine nodded in relief.

"While I was there," continued Denny, "the Blackfoot messenger returned from the Sioux. He said that the Sioux were angry with the Blackfoot decision and that they would attack the Blackfoot after they killed the Americans. Crowfoot asked me if the Mounties would assist the Blackfoot should the Sioux carry through on their threat. I told them that if the Sioux crossed the line and attacked the Blackfoot without cause, we were bound to help them, they being subjects of this country and having the right to the same protection as any other subjects."

"Well said," agreed Irvine.

"Crowfoot then spoke to me. He said, 'We all see that the day is coming when the buffalo will all be killed, and we shall have nothing more to live on, and then you will come into our camp and see the poor Blackfoot starving. I know that the heart of the white solider will be sorry for us, and you will tell the Great White Mother, who will not let her children starve. We are getting shut in. The Crees are coming into our country from the north and the white men from the south and east. They are all destroying our means of living, but still, although we plainly see those days coming, we will not join the Sioux against the whites, but will depend on you to help us.' He finished by advising me that the Blackfoot would provide 2000 warriors to help us if necessary.

A.G. Irvine (1837–1916), third commissioner of the NWMP, joined the force after the march and led it during the North-West Rebellion.

≈✕≈

"I thanked them for their offer and reminded them that if they kept the peace, they would always find us their good friends and willing to do anything for their good. They promised to do nothing without letting us know and asking our advice."

Denny's report eventually reached Queen Victoria, who forwarded a personal message of thanks to the Blackfoot chief for his people's loyalty.

Sitting Bull crossed the Medicine Line in the spring of 1877. He traveled north near the Cypress Hills and Fort Walsh, where Major James Walsh was in command. Walsh and a handful of men found the Sioux camp near Pinto Horse Butte.*

As they approached it, Sioux braves surrounded them. Walsh knew one of them.

"Spotted Eagle, my friend," he said, and he stepped forward to embrace the man.

"Long Lance, it is good to see you," replied the Sans Arc chief, calling Walsh the name by which the Sioux knew him.

"We are looking for Sitting Bull," said Walsh. "Is he here? We wish to speak to him."

"This is the camp of Sitting Bull. It is good you are here for he wishes to hear what you have to say. Come," said Spotted Eagle, as he led the Mounties into the camp.

"You know, Long Lance, no white man has ever dared to enter the camp of Sitting Bull. And with good reason, for he would not leave it alive," Spotted Eagle stated.

Walsh replied without missing a beat.

"I do not fear for my safety. I am a Mountie, a representative of the Great White Mother's council to the east. I've got a job to do." *And, by God, it'll be done,* he added to himself.

The Mounties were directed to a large lodge at the center of the camp. Surrounding it were several Sioux, whom Walsh thought were the band's headmen. They stood, and the shortest of them limped towards the Mounties. He took Sergeant McCutcheon's hand and shook it vigorously.

"I am Sitting Bull. Welcome to my camp."

The surprised sergeant searched for an answer.

"Ummm, glad to be here, chief."

---

*Read a full account of the story of Sitting Bull in Canada, published by Folklore Publishing.

This illustration, Sitting Bull on Dominion Territory, appeared in the *Canadian Illustrated News* in September 1877. Sitting Bull's journey north was a long and bloody one. The Sioux chief desired peace, but American soldiers and settlers pushed onto traditional Sioux territory and forced him to defend his people's way of life. When gold was discovered in the Black Hills, the American government allowed prospectors into the region in defiance of its treaty obligations with the Sioux. That decision caused violent warfare on the mid-western plains. After decimating the Seventh Cavalry at the Battle of the Little Bighorn, Sitting Bull and his followers were pursued relentlessly by General Nelson Miles and the Fifth Cavalry. Unable to hunt and facing starvation, Sitting Bull led his people to the Great White Mother's land, where he hoped for a reservation and peace.

Walsh stepped forward.

"I am Major James Walsh, the Queen's head chief in these parts." The scout Léveillé translated.

"Ahh, Meejure, the one called Long Lance," replied Sitting Bull.

"I've come to tell you about the Great White Mother's law," said Walsh.

"Please tell, for I wish to hear."

"You know you are in the land of the Great White Mother?"

"Yes. We know it well. I was raised in these parts with the Red River Half-breeds. My grandfather fought with the Great White Father."

"We've got laws here that must be obeyed by whites and Indians alike. There's no killing and no stealing. And that includes horses. Women and children are not to be harmed. Most importantly, you are not to go back to the United States and wage war upon the Americans and then return across the border to Canada. Should that happen, the Americans will surely not be your only enemies."

"I buried my weapons before I crossed the Medicine Line," said Sitting Bull. "My heart is no longer bad."

"I am glad to hear it. Obey the laws, and no harm will come to you," advised Walsh.

Throughout the summer of 1877, the Sioux did just that. Mostly, they remained Walsh's concern because Commissioner Macleod was busy with arrangements for Treaty 7 with the Blackfoot. Along with Lieutenant-Governor David Laird, he was appointed as a commissioner to negotiate with the Natives in the unsurrendered territory in the southern North-West Territories. It was an important assignment. The Dominion government had negotiated treaties that gave it control over all the southern North-West Territories from the Great Lakes and almost to the Rocky Mountains. Only the territory controlled by the Blackfoot Confederacy was unsecured. Plans for white settlement and railway expansion demanded that matter be addressed.

In early September, 1877, Laird joined Commissioner Macleod at Fort Macleod, his command headquarters. The lieutenant-governor was immediately impressed by the Mounties' relationship with the Natives.

"I cannot speak too highly of the kind manner in which the officers and men of the Mounted Police at Fort Macleod treat their Indian visitors," he reported to Ottawa. "Though the red man is somewhat intrusive, I never heard a harsh word employed in asking him to retire. The beneficial effects of this treatment, of the exclusion of intoxicants from the country and of impartial administration of justice to whites and Indians alike were apparent in all my interviews with the Indians. They always spoke of the officers of the police in the highest terms, and of the commander of the force, Lieutenant-Colonel Macleod as their great benefactor."

At Crowfoot's insistence, the treaty council was moved from Fort Macleod to the neutral setting of Blackfoot Crossing on the Bow River. Blackfoot and Mounties arrived during the first weeks of September, and on the 17th, a ceremonial shot from a nine-pounder opened the council. The chiefs approached the council tent and were introduced to the treaty commissioners. Headmen and other braves followed and sat near the tent.

"Last year the Great White Mother's government promised you that commissioners would invite you to make treaty," said Laird. "We are now here to discuss the terms of that treaty. But we see that all your people are not yet here, so we will adjourn to give them time to arrive. In the meantime, rations will be available for those who want them."

Among those not yet at the council grounds were Chief Red Crow and his Blood followers. The concern was that he might not come to the council because he was not as supportive of treaty as other Blackfoot. The Natives agreed to the delay, but

The Blackfoot Treaty (No.7) by A.B. Stapleton. Crowfoot is speaking, while Commissioner Macleod and Lieutenant Governor Laird listen.

~⚬✕⚬~

Crowfoot refused any rations or gifts until he heard the terms of the treaty.

When the council reconvened, the Blood still absent, Laird again addressed those assembled:

> In a very few years, the buffalo will probably be all destroyed, and for this reason the Great White Mother wishes to help you to live in the future in some other way. She wishes you to

allow her white children to come and live on your land and raise cattle, and should you agree to this she will assist you to raise cattle and grain, and thus give you the means of living when the buffalo are no more. She will also pay you and your children money every year, which you can spend as you please.

Laird gave more details on the rations, money and goods that treaty would bring, and the Natives retired to discuss the offer. Most realized that the buffalo would disappear and that some other means of livelihood would soon be necessary. Crowfoot was among that number. He knew that making treaty would mean a loss of territory and independence, but there seemed to be no alternative. Still, he was not willing to agree to the lieutenant-governor's offer until Red Crow arrived. He wanted the Blackfoot to be a united front.

Red Crow finally arrived, and when he learned the details of the treaty, he discussed it with his people. While some dissent was voiced, Red Crow agreed to make treaty if Crowfoot and his people did also. On September 21, Crowfoot addressed the council with his decision:

While I speak, be kind and patient. I have to speak for my people, who are numerous and who rely upon me to follow that course which in the future will tend to their good. The plains are large and wide. We are the children of the plains, it is our home, and the buffalo has been our food always. I hope you look upon the Siksika, Blood and Sarcee as your children now, and that you will be indulgent and charitable to them. They all expect me to speak now for them, and I trust the good spirits will put into their breasts to be a good people—into the minds of men, women and children, and their future generations.

The advice given me and my people has proved to be very good. If the police had not come to the country, where would

*we all be now? Bad men and whiskey were killing us all so
fast that very few, indeed, of us would have been left today.
The Police have protected us as the feathers of the bird protect it from the frosts of winter. I wish them all good, and trust
that all our hearts will increase in goodness from this time forward. I am satisfied. I will sign the treaty.*

Crowfoot's promise was dispassionate, but the good of his
people and what he saw of the future convinced him that treaty
was necessary. Nevertheless, even his lukewarm agreement
would have been unlikely had he not trusted Macleod and the
Red Coats. The efforts of the force to remove the whiskey
traders and ensure equality before the law gave Crowfoot and
the Blackfoot the confidence to cede their lands in return for
the protection and assistance of the Dominion government.

Macleod was subsequently charged with negotiating reservations, and although Treaty 7 still had to be signed, the North-
West Mounted Police had done its job. It had secured the West
and opened it for peaceful white settlement. When Prime Minister John A. Macdonald first imagined the force in the late
1860s, he hoped for nothing more.

Epilogue

THE NORTH-WEST MOUNTED POLICE faced other challenges in the decade following the signing of Treaty 7. Substantial white settlement did not occur until the 1890s, so the Mounties' activities revolved around the Natives. The decade witnessed the decimation of the buffalo herds, and many Natives found it difficult to make the transition to the settled life of the reservation. The Dominion government provided little assistance; it was often parsimonious and patronizing in its dealings with the Natives and tardy in its treaty obligations.

While Sitting Bull and his Sioux followers remained in Canada, the force was responsible for ensuring that they were peaceful. That no major incidents occurred involving the Sioux was due mostly Major James Walsh's efforts. He formed a close friendship with Sitting Bull and earned the respect of the chief and his people. The Sioux returned to the United States in 1881, when it became clear that the Dominion government would not provide them with food or a reservation.

In 1885, the North-West Rebellion (or Second Riel Rebellion) erupted. The Métis who supported this second rebellion tried to win the Blackfoot's support to improve their chances of victory. The Blackfoot considered the offer of their one-time enemies, an indication of the difficult years that followed the signing of Treaty 7. When the new lieutenant-governor, Edgar Dewdney, visited Crowfoot upon the eruption of violence, the Blackfoot chief told him he would remain loyal to the Great White Mother. Although Crowfoot was not as confident in the Dominion government as he had been a decade before, he expressed that his confidence was borne of the goodwill fostered by the North-West Mounted Police. Mounties fought in the 1885 Rebellion, which was ultimately quashed.

As for some of the men in the force:

Frederick Bagley resigned with the rank of Staff Sergeant after a 25-year career with the force. He later served in the Canadian army and fought in both the South African War and World War I, resigning with the rank of major.

Cecil Denny resigned as an inspector in 1882 and thereafter worked in a variety of jobs, including Indian agent and fire ranger before he settled into a career as provincial archivist of Alberta. In 1922, he inherited his father's title and became the sixth baronet of Tralee Castle.

George French, in his official 1874 report, offered his heartfelt thanks to the Dominion government "for having placed me in a position, which entitles me to claim that I was a member of a corps, which performed one of the most extraordinary marches on record." After his (forced) resignation in 1876, he returned to England and subsequently served in the British army in India and Australia. He was knighted for his service to the empire and retired in 1902 as Major-General Sir George French. He visited Canada in 1906 and toured the North-West Mounted Police force headquarters at Regina. He always maintained that the march was less of an endurance than claimed by many of the men.

Henri Julien returned to the *Canadian Illustrated News* after his departure from the North-West Mounted Police in late 1874. He enjoyed a successful career as an illustrator and cartoonist until his death in 1908.

James Macleod resigned his command in 1880, likely under pressure from Prime Minister John A. Macdonald but continued to serve as a magistrate for the North-West Territories. In 1887, he was appointed to the Supreme Court of the North-West Territories.

Sam Steele was promoted to commissioned officer in 1878, given command of Fort Qu'Appelle in 1879 and promoted to superintendent in 1885. He was later responsible for maintaining order in the Yukon during the Klondike gold rush at the turn of the century. He commanded forces during the South African War and trained men during World War I.

Jerry Potts continued to assist the force in its relations with the Native peoples after his invaluable service to the force in the years leading up to the signing of Treaty 7. His efforts helped to ensure that the Blackfoot remained neutral during the 1885 Rebellion. He worked as a guide, scout and interpreter for the North-West Mounted Police for 22 years.

James Walsh displeased the Dominion government with his handling of the Sitting Bull affair, and the man some called "Sitting Bull's Boss" was reassigned in 1880. He resigned in 1883 and went into the coal business. But, during the Klondike gold rush, he was appointed Commissioner of the Yukon.

Notes on Sources

THE DIALOGUE IN THIS BOOK is true to the sources, and the accounts described are fictionalized as little as possible.

Butler, William F. *The Great Lone Land*. 1872. Reprint ed. Edmonton: Hurtig Ltd., 1968.

Chambers, Ernest J. *The Royal North-West Mounted Police: A Corps History*. 1906. Reprint ed. Toronto: Coles Publishing, 1972.

Commissioners of the Royal North-West Mounted Police. *Opening Up the West: Being the Official Reports to Parliament of the Activities of the Royal North-West Mounted Police Force from 1874-1881*. 1881. Reprint ed. Toronto: Coles Publishing, 1973.

Crauford-Lewis, Michael. *Macleod of the Mounties*. Ottawa: Golden Dog Press, 1999.

Cruise, David & Alison Griffiths. *The Great Adventure: How the Mounties Conquered the West*. Toronto: Viking, 1996.

Denny, Cecil. *March of the Mounties*. 1932. Reprint ed. Surrey: Heritage House, 1994.

Hollihan, Tony. *Great Chiefs, Volume II*. Edmonton: Folklore Publishing, 2002.

———. *Sitting Bull in Canada*. Edmonton: Folklore Publishing, 2001.

Julien, Henri. *The North West Expedition—1874 of the North-West Mounted Police: Diary of Henri Julien*. Calgary: Glenbow Archives, M611.

Macleod, R.C. "The North-West Mounted Police, 1873-1905." Ph.D., Duke University, 1971.

———. *The North West Mounted Police, 1873-1919*. Ottawa: Canadian Historical Association, 1978.

Morris, Alexander. *The Treaties of Canada with the Indians*. 1880. Reprint ed. Toronto: Coles, 1979.

Steele, Sam. *Fort Years in Canada*. 1915. Reprint ed. Toronto: Prospero Books, 2000.

Turner, John. *The North-West Mounted Police, 1873-1893*. Ottawa: King's Printer, 1950.

Wallace, Jim. *A Double Duty*. Winnipeg: Bunker to Bunker Books, 1997.

Author Bio

DR. TONY HOLLIHAN is an educator, author and historian who has held a lifelong fascination with the historical and sometimes mythic figures of North America. Born in St. John's, Newfoundland, Dr. Hollihan developed his interest in history at an early age and pursued it at Memorial University of Newfoundland and later at the University of Alberta. He has a Ph.D. in the History of Education and a Masters degree in Canadian and American history. He continues to share his interest in history through teaching and writing. He is the author of several books in Folklore Publishing's Legends series, including *Kootenai Brown*, *Sitting Bull in Canada*, *Great Chiefs, Volumes I and II*, and *Mountain Men: Frontier Adventurers Alone Against the Wilderness*. Dr. Hollihan lives in Edmonton (where he dreams of the ocean) with his wife Laureen and their three sons.

FOLK LORE PUBLISHING

Where history comes to life

If you enjoyed *The Mounties March West*, you'll love these other great historical narratives by Tony Hollihan...

Coming Soon
Disasters of Western Canada: Courage Amidst the Chaos
by Tony Hollihan

From deadly floods and blizzards to tragic coal-mining accidents, Western Canada has had its share of disasters. A must-read for anyone with a penchant for powerful human dramas, this collection tells poignant stories of devastation, loss of life and remarkable courage in the face of adversity.

$10.95 US • $14.95 CDN • ISBN 1-894864-13-1 • 5.25" x 8.25"
232 pages

Mountain Men: Frontier Adventurers Alone Against the Wilderness
by Tony Hollihan

Travel back to the days of the wild frontier with this entertaining series of accounts about the real men behind some of the West's most popular wilderness heroes. Tony Hollihan explores the colorful lives of eight mountain men, including Davy Crockett, Daniel Boone, Jedidiah Smith and Kit Carson.

$10.95 US • $14.95 CDN • ISBN 1-894864-09-3 • 5.25" x 8.25"
224 pages

Crazy Horse: Warrior Spirit of the Sioux
by Tony Hollihan

Best known for his role in defeating General Custer at the Little Bighorn, Crazy Horse was a visionary leader who fought tirelessly to preserve the Sioux tradition. This engaging story recounts his transformation from a solitary boy nicknamed "Curly" into a legendary war chief.

$10.95 US • $14.95 CDN • ISBN 1-894864-08-5 • 5.25" x 8.25"
232 pages

Great Chiefs, Volume I
by Tony Hollihan

Read about the legendary Native chiefs who guided their people through the most turbulent chapter in their history, the arrival of the white man on their land. Included in this volume are portrayals of Sitting Bull, Chief Joseph, Quanah Parker, Red Cloud, Louis Riel and Sequoyah.

$10.95 US • $14.95 CDN • ISBN 1-894864-03-4 • 5.25" x 8.25" 320 pages

Great Chiefs, Volume II
by Tony Hollihan

Tony Hollihan relates more fascinating tales of the courageous chiefs and warriors of North America's western Native tribes who battled valiantly against the growing tide of European settlement on their lands. The stories of Geronimo, Tecumseh, Crowfoot, Plenty Coups, Wovoka and Crazy Horse are featured.

$10.95 US • $14.95 CDN • ISBN 1-894864-07-7 • 5.25" x 8.25" 320 pages

Sitting Bull in Canada
by Tony Hollihan

Follow the story of Sitting Bull as he retreats into Canada after the Battle of the Little Bighorn and begins an improbable friendship with the celebrated Mountie, Major James Walsh. Tony Hollihan narrates the tale of Sitting Bull's determined attempts to preserve the traditional Sioux way of life.

$10.95 US • $14.95 CDN • ISBN 1-894864-02-6 • 5.25" x 8.25" 288 pages

Look for books from Folklore Publishing at your local bookseller and newsstand or contact the distributor, Lone Pine Publishing, directly. In the U.S. call 1-800-518-3541. In Canada, call 1-800-661-9017.